A Farmer's Daughter

Recipes from a Mennonite Kitchen

DAWN STOLTZFUS

Revell

a division of Baker Publishing Group
Grand Rapids, Michigan

Published by Revell
a division of Baker Publishing Group
P.O. Box 6287, Grand Rapids, MI 49516-6287
www.revellbooks.com

Printed in the United States of America

Library of Congress Cataloging-in-Publication Data
Stoltzfus, Dawn, 1947–
        A farmer's daughter: recipes from a Mennonite kitchen / Dawn Stoltzfus.
            p.   cm.
        Includes index.
        ISBN 978-0-8007-2091-9 (pbk.)
        1. Mennonite cooking. I. Title.
    TX721.S755 2012
    641.5′66—dc23   2012017994

12   13   14   15   16   17   18   7   6   5   4   3   2

This labor of love is dedicated to my mother Carol Falb, who put up with way too many open cupboard doors and messy days in the kitchen. She still tells me, "I don't know how one person can make such a mess." I don't know either. All I know is that if she had not let that happen, this cookbook would not be a reality. Thanks, Mom, for teaching me the basics and letting me be adventurous in your kitchen. You have inspired me over and over; I am still learning from you and your creativity!

Contents

Acknowledgments

To the love of my life, my amazing husband, who rescued the kitchen from piles of dishes multiple times late at night, who tasted more food than he ever wanted to, who played Mr. Mom so that I could think while working on this project, and who originally birthed this idea of a cookbook in my heart.

To Blyss and her sweet family, who faithfully let me drop my little munchkins off at their home once a week to be entertained. This allowed me to sit in my house in complete silence and with peace of mind to work on this project. My boys have fallen in love with you!

To Sierra, who was my substitute child care provider and always loved my boys so well. I knew they were in good hands when they were with you.

To all my friends who tasted lots of food and gave me honest opinions about whether or not the recipes were keepers.

To Bridgette, who, second to my mom, has shared more kitchen time with me than any other person I know. You did it again as I raced to the finish line with ninety recipes to tweak and pregnant as the day is long. Your mad skills came through again. Thanks, BB!

I am surrounded by amazing cooks in my life, women who love to cook and create beauty all around them. So to all of my foodie friends whom I have shared kitchen time with, made great memories with, and ended up washing far too many dishes with: Cheryl, Jenelle, Rita, Emily, Sandy, Jess, Anita, and Sheree, you have all spurred me on this journey. I am very grateful to you for teaching me and inspiring me!

To Andrea, who waltzed into my life by accident, per say. Ten years ago I would never have dreamed I would have an editor someday, but here you are, and you have become my friend in this process. You have helped me become excited for this project, with your phone calls just to say thank you, your emails telling of recipes tried long before the manuscript had even been edited, and your admission that the Pumpkin Cinnamon Rolls you made for your church bake sale never made it there. You have done more to my soul than I think you will ever know—thank you for believing in me!

Introduction

I grew up in a real farmhouse kitchen in Ohio, where I began creating recipes for our family of six at the age of sixteen. My father was a bi-vocational Mennonite pastor and farmer, so we had a busy life that included ministry and a demanding farm. We raised our own beef, had fresh milk, and for a season had a brood of chickens my mother named and gathered eggs from.

As a young woman away from the farm, I missed all those fresh ingredients and home cooked meals—and I figured I wasn't alone. I opened a store in a western suburb of Washington, DC, called The Farmer's Wife, named in honor of my mother. The Farmer's Wife specialized in things you would find in a farm kitchen: real butter, farm-fresh milk in glass bottles, and all kinds of baked goodness. Running it for more than four years taught me so much about people, how important food is to our families and relationships, and what recipes make people smile. Though I sold the store in order to raise our young family, I've remembered and incorporated those lessons into my life, and into this collection of recipes.

My life is rich, but not because my parents had lots of money when we were growing up. It is rich because of the relationships that have been forged through good and hard times. As I reflect about what draws people together, I am struck by how a plate of food, whether it is a simple pasta dish or a delicious steak, plain green beans or green beans almondine, a slice of plain white bread or a piece of crusty artisan sourdough, a plain chocolate chip cookie or peanut butter whoopie pie, has a way of bringing people together. Relationships are formed over food, and sharing meals with the ones you love has a way of opening our lives up to each other.

We use food to live. We use it to celebrate. When you are in a home where you feel welcomed, the food seems to offer confirmation of how you feel. Your senses come alive and your soul is at rest. We gather around food to process life, and throw a party just because there is good food. Rarely do we get together with a group of people without food. We gather around it as a family during happy and sad times. Recently, as our family grieved over the passing of several members, we shared meals together and something good happened. We talked, we reminisced, we laughed, and we cried—and we healed in ways we could not have expected, all over food prepared by people who cared for us.

This cookbook is designed to offer simple but wholesome food along with classic recipes that are great to serve your family or to entertain guests. It offers practical tips for entertaining guests with ease and personal stories from my family—and will hopefully spark ideas about creating your own family legacy with recipes. Whether you like to cook—or you just like to eat well—I hope you will find simple recipes here that will "wow" your family.

Dawn

1

Appetizers, Dips, and Beverages

My mother has a wonderful array of appetizers she prepares for all of us who can make it home on Christmas Eve. Over the years she has developed the recipes to our family's liking. My mother faithfully creates a wonderful presentation with her amazing kitchen skills. My siblings and I all have our "own favorite" things we like to see on her buffet table. I know my brother Mike's favorite is the pink jello fluff. My only sister Jenelle and I adore the layered Mexican dip, and my younger brother Gary's favorite is all things shrimp. This is such a fun gathering of our hearts as we gather around in the little kitchen, wait for Dad to bless the food, and then dig in and introduce our spouses and children to the things we love on that table. We experience our mother's love as she so graciously prepares things just for us.

Traditions remind us of years gone by and of special times shared, but they also pull us into today and make us want to stay in that place of warm love! Be intentional about the traditions that are uniquely your family's. They give us a sense of security, a sense of belonging. The world is cold out there and what a better place for our children, whether young or old, to return to than that beautiful place we call home. Fill your home with beauty, with music, with candles, with good food, and with traditions that will continue to warm their hearts long after they leave.

Simple things grab my attention, pull me in, and make me feel welcome, like I want to stay for a long time! Soft music, the warm glow of a candle, my son's tiny arms wrapped tightly around my neck, summer rain, a hint of rosemary on the grill, that first daffodil that peeps its head through the ground, a campfire, fresh baked brownies, a bouquet of hydrangeas, maple icing, a beautifully decorated luncheon table, sweet time with Jesus, a very hot cup of coffee in the first thirty minutes I am awake. All these are little—but BIG.

This is how I view garnishes; they are simple but pull you in. Every time I experience someone's creative work in the form of a garnish, it makes the salad, the breakfast, the soup, the entrée, the muffin, or the cup of coffee so much better.

Garnishes take time, but I am learning to build in a little extra time when I cook so I can add these little touches. It is so worth it, and your guests will feel loved.

Here are a few simple ideas:

Fresh herbs snipped and sprinkled over a quiche
A dab of whipped cream and a raspberry to top a muffin
Whipped cream with chocolate drizzles, crushed peppermint, or cinnamon on coffee
A whole orange slice with a strawberry on top to crown an entrée plate
A sprig of rosemary and mint lying on a dinner plate
A mint sprig in a glass of garden mint tea
A strong four-inch rosemary sprig threaded with red and green grapes on a brunch plate
Fresh or dried herbs sprinkled on soup

Cranberry Salsa

2 cups	fresh cranberries
1 cup	water
1 cup	orange juice
¾ cup	raw or white sugar
⅓ cup	fresh cilantro, minced
½ cup	green bell pepper, diced fine
1–2	green onions, minced
⅛ tsp.	red pepper flakes
2 tsp.	cumin
	zest from 1 lime
	juice from 1 lime

Combine cranberries, water, orange juice, and sugar in a saucepan over high heat and boil for 10 minutes. Let cool. Stir cilantro, green pepper, and green onions into cooled cranberry sauce. Add red pepper flakes, cumin, lime zest, and lime juice. Stir well. Yields 3 cups.

Place the salsa in a pretty jar with the instructions to serve Cranberry Salsa over Cream Cheese attached as a beautiful hostess gift!

🐦 **And Another Thing . . . And Another Thing . . .** Fresh cranberries are hard to find after January, so I like to stock up over the holidays. I place the extra bags in my freezer for use at a later date. All year long I can make cranberry salsa; use cranberries for decoration in pretty, clear glass containers; and thread short skewers with cranberries to place in a drinking glass as a beverage garnish.

Cranberry Salsa over Cream Cheese

This is such a pretty dish to serve at Christmas. It is cranberry red with hints of green from the green pepper and cilantro.

8 oz.   cream cheese, softened
1 cup   Cranberry Salsa (see recipe above)
            crackers of your choice

Spread cream cheese evenly onto a serving plate, shaping it into a rectangle, and spread Cranberry Salsa over evenly. Serve with your favorite crackers. Serves 8.

French Pecan Cheese Spread

8 oz.	cream cheese, softened
1 Tbsp.	dried chives
1 Tbsp.	red onion, diced
1 tsp.	garlic powder
¼ cup	salted butter
¼ cup	brown sugar, packed
2 tsp.	Worcestershire sauce
1 cup	pecans, toasted and chopped fine
	assorted crackers

In a small bowl, combine cream cheese, chives, red onion, and garlic powder. Transfer to a serving plate and shape into a rectangle.

In a small saucepan, combine butter, brown sugar, and Worcestershire sauce. Cook and stir over medium heat for 3 minutes. Remove from heat and add pecans. Chill in refrigerator for 10 minutes, then spoon nut mixture over cream cheese. Serve with crackers. Serves 8.

Pesto Cream Cheese Spread

This recipe is S.I.M.P.L.E. You can wrap it in foil and throw it on the grill while the grill is preheating, and by the time you are ready to put your main entrée on the grill you will have a simple appetizer ready to eat. When fresh basil and tomatoes are at their peak, this is a wonderful, inexpensive appetizer.

8 oz.	cream cheese
3 Tbsp.	pesto
½ cup	grape tomatoes—cut in half
¼ cup	Italian blend or mozzarella cheese, shredded
2 Tbsp.	pine nuts or walnuts, chopped
	variety of crackers
	red and green bell pepper strips

Place cream cheese on a piece of foil that is large enough to close. Spread pesto on top of cream cheese, then add tomatoes, shredded cheese, and nuts. Close foil, sealing well. Bake in oven at 350°F for 15–18 minutes, or place on the grill for 8–10 minutes, until center of the cream cheese is warm. Serve with crackers and pepper strips. Serves 6–8.

Lime Fruit Dip

The red and green of the fruit make this particularly pretty at Christmas and also at the beginning of strawberry season. There is something remarkable about fresh, just-picked, juicy strawberries. This dip needs no other fruit to make a glorious treat.

1 cup	whipping cream
½ cup	powdered sugar
8 oz.	cream cheese
6 oz.	lime yogurt
½ tsp.	lime zest
1 tsp.	lime juice
	fresh strawberries and kiwi

In a small mixing bowl, beat whipping cream until soft peaks form, then add powdered sugar. In another bowl, beat cream cheese until smooth, then stir in yogurt, lime zest, and lime juice. Fold in whipped cream. Serve with strawberries and kiwi. Yields 2½ cups.

🐦 **And Another Thing . . . And Another Thing . . .** A creative way to serve kiwi is to cut it into half dollar circles and wedges. It gives a nice presentation to your plate.

Hot Pizza Dip

8 oz.	cream cheese, softened
1 cup	Greek yogurt or sour cream
1 cup	pizza sauce
1 tsp.	basil
1 tsp.	oregano
2	garlic cloves, minced
pinch	red pepper
1½ cups	Mexican blend cheese, shredded
½ cup	red or green bell pepper, chopped fine
¼ cup	onion, chopped fine
½ cup	pepperoni slices

Preheat oven to 350°F. In a mixing bowl combine cream cheese, yogurt, pizza sauce, basil, oregano, garlic, and red pepper, and mix well. Place mixture in an 8 x 8 baking dish. Sprinkle with cheese, then chopped pepper, onion, and pepperoni. Bake for 20–25 minutes or until bubbly.

Serve warm with breadsticks, green pepper strips, or tortilla chips.

Tomato, Olive, and Cheese on Rosemary Skewers

1 pint	cherry tomatoes, washed
1 cup	kalamata olives, no pits
4–6 oz.	mozzarella cheese, cubed
12–16 (6 in.) stems	rosemary, bottom half of leaves removed
2 Tbsp.	olive oil
2 tsp.	balsamic vinegar
4 leaves	fresh basil, diced small
	fresh cracked pepper and salt

Thread 1 tomato, 1 olive, and 1 cheese chunk onto the bottom half of a rosemary stem. Repeat. Lay stems on a cookie sheet and sprinkle with oil and vinegar; add basil, pepper, and salt. Chill until ready to serve. Yields 12–16 appetizers.

Peppered Sugar Pecans

These are wonderful served with apple slices and cheese. Serve on an appetizer platter or toss them into a salad. You decide how you would like to eat them. Who knows? You might end up eating them all yourself as a snack.

1 Tbsp.	salted butter
3 Tbsp.	brown sugar
1 Tbsp.	Worcestershire sauce
½ tsp.	cinnamon
¼ tsp.	red pepper flakes (or more if you like hot)
2 cups	pecan halves

Melt butter in a skillet over medium heat. In a small bowl, mix together brown sugar, Worcestershire sauce, cinnamon, and red pepper flakes; add pecans. Pour pecan mixture into skillet. Cook, stirring frequently, about 5 minutes or until pecans smell fragrant. Make sure they don't burn. Remove from heat and spread pecans out on a cookie sheet to cool about 1 hour.

🐌 **And Another Thing . . . And Another Thing . . .** These pecans store in an airtight container in the refrigerator for up to 4 weeks, or can be frozen up to 6 months. I like to make a double batch and place half in the freezer for the next party or for a salad at a later time.

Stuffed Mushrooms

Appetizers can be complicated, but this has to be the least time-consuming appetizer I have ever made.

8 oz.	fresh white mushrooms
3–4 oz.	Monterey or cheddar cheese, diced
	salt and pepper
1 Tbsp.	olive oil

Preheat oven broiler. Wash mushrooms and de-stem. Place mushrooms on an ungreased cookie sheet stem side up; put a cheese chunk into each one. Sprinkle mushrooms with salt and pepper, then drizzle with olive oil.

Broil for 5–7 minutes or until cheese is bubbly and brown. Serve immediately. Serves 4–6.

> ✒ And Another Thing . . . And Another Thing . . . I also like to use an herb-flavored cheddar cheese for this recipe. Any cheese will work, and will have your mushroom lovers raving!

Sausage and Rye Toasts

My mother makes these every year for our Christmas Eve appetizer extravaganza. These salty, tasty bites of goodness spell LOVE to the Falb siblings. My husband, on the other hand, looks at them as if they are "not all that." It might be because he is not a big fan of rye, but it could be that they don't communicate love to him the way they do to us. Why don't you try them and see what you think? What's most important here is not whether these make the cut into your box of "collectable recipes," but to think about the recipes from home that you love. What are the ways you communicate to your children—young or old—that traditions matter? Allow these family recipes to become gifts you give your children long after you have changed their last diaper. Name the traditions, own them, and help make memories for years to come. I don't think my mother set out to make this specific recipe a tradition. The fact that she is carrying it on long after we have left her nest is what makes these salty, tasty yummies so delish!

1 lb.	ground beef
1 lb.	ground sausage
¾–1 lb.	American cheese, cubed
1 tsp.	dried oregano
½ tsp.	garlic powder
1 lb. loaf	small party rye bread (often found by your grocery store's deli)

Preheat oven to 350°F. Brown ground beef and sausage in a skillet. Drain. Add cheese and seasonings, and stir until cheese is melted. Spread 1 tablespoon of mixture onto each piece of rye bread. Place on cookie sheets. Bake for 5 minutes. Yields 32–36 little open-faced sandwiches.

Double Decker Creamy Finger Gelatin

This is for the kiddos, but beware: they will disappear when the "big kids" are in the room too. My aunt Mary used to make these for us kids every Christmas. No matter how much she made, I don't think she ever went home with leftovers. Raspberry gelatin is my all-time favorite!

3 (3 oz.) pkgs.	flavored gelatin
3 cups	boiling water
1 cup	heavy whipping cream

Dissolve gelatin in boiling water. Allow to cool for 10–15 minutes. Add cream and stir. Pour into a 9 x 13 pan and refrigerate. This gelatin will separate as it sets up and look like you made it in 2 layers. Refrigerate for 6 hours. Cut into 1-inch pieces and enjoy! Serves 16–18.

🐦 **And Another Thing . . . And Another Thing . . .** For a fun presentation, serve bite-size squares in a large vintage canning jar. For even more fun, make two batches—at Christmas use strawberry gelatin for one and lime gelatin for the other, and layer the colors in the glass jar. For a Fourth of July party use raspberry and blueberry gelatin, and for a fall party use lemon and orange.

Butterscotch Steamer

¼ cup	salted butter
½ cup	brown sugar
1 qt.	milk
4 cups	double strength brewed coffee or espresso
pinch	cinnamon

Over medium-low heat, melt butter in saucepan and add brown sugar. Add milk, stirring, just until hot. Do not boil. Remove from heat and stir in hot coffee. Pour into mugs and sprinkle with cinnamon. Serves 4.

Caramel Whipped Cream

This is a great addition to an evening cup of coffee. It's a glorious dessert without too many calories. When served in a clear glass mug, the whipping cream looks so pretty as it melts down over the coffee. Whenever I make this and sip it from a clear coffee mug, it takes me back to the days when I was vacationing with some friends in Antigua, Guatemala. Oh, they know how to make gorgeous coffee drinks! It is an art, and it was so delightful to end our days in that coffee shop, sipping on a specially handcrafted coffee and sharing in deep, heartfelt conversation.

1 cup	whipping cream
1 Tbsp.	brown sugar, packed
1 Tbsp.	powdered sugar
2 Tbsp.	caramel sauce, room temperature
	additional caramel sauce for drizzling

Beat whipping cream until soft peaks form, add sugars; beat again just until mixed and add caramel sauce. Beat until stiff peaks form. Drop a tablespoon or two on a hot, steamy cup of coffee, drizzle with additional caramel sauce, and enjoy. Yields 14 tablespoons.

You can refrigerate the leftovers; however, it does not hold up very well for a long time, 3–4 days maximum. If you don't need this much whipped cream, prepare half the recipe.

Chai Tea Latte

It is so fun to serve up a specialty drink to anyone who will drink it with me. I so enjoy sitting down and sharing a cozy cup of something warm with another kindred spirit. I have a hard time wrapping my mind around what heaven will be like, but I think there is nothing in life more delicious than sharing my soul with another and having them do the same. Those moments to me are bits of heaven, and when they quickly pass and that very real ache returns, I am reminded that this is not our home, and we really do "press on for the prize" (see Phil. 4:13–14). So here's to one more yummy, steaming hot drink to share with someone or sip alone as you spend time with your Creator.

4 cups	water
4 small	black tea or Lipton tea bags
4 whole	cloves
¼ tsp.	ground cinnamon
pinch	ground ginger
⅓ cup	brown sugar
2 cups	milk
	whipped cream and cinnamon (to garnish)

Bring water to a boil; add tea bags and cloves. Reduce heat and simmer for 5 minutes. Remove tea bags and cloves. Add cinnamon, ginger, and sugar; mix well. Add milk, and heat just until hot, stirring frequently. Remove from heat. Do not allow to simmer on the stove once heated. Garnish with whipped cream and cinnamon, if desired. Serves 3–4.

Pumpkin Spice Latte

Last fall, after traveling seven hours with two babies, I arrived home in Ohio to that wonderful place called my mother's kitchen and was welcomed by this delicious latte. Every warm, cozy emotion that could be evoked oozed from within me, and I felt that sense of belonging we experience when someone we love serves us such yummies after a long day. My mother has a whole array of seasonal drinks and this one is always served in the fall.

4 cups	milk
¼ cup	canned pumpkin
¼ cup	brown sugar
1 tsp.	cinnamon
2 cups	strong, hot brewed coffee
	whipped cream and cinnamon (to garnish)

In a medium saucepan, stir together milk, pumpkin, and sugar. Heat over low heat until steaming. Add cinnamon and coffee. Pour into mugs and garnish with whipped cream and cinnamon. You can also pour into a blender and blend for 30 seconds to make it frothy. Serves 4.

Maple Hot Chocolate

⅓ cup	pure maple syrup
1 Tbsp.	cocoa powder
⅛ tsp.	salt
¼ cup	water
1 Tbsp.	salted butter
4 cups	milk
1 tsp.	maple extract
8 lg.	marshmallows

In a small saucepan, combine maple syrup, cocoa powder, salt, water, and butter; stir well and bring to a boil. Stir in milk and heat just until hot; do not scorch. Remove from heat and add maple extract. Pour into mugs and top with marshmallows. Serves 4.

Creamy Hot Cocoa

I remember my mother standing at her stove stirring this wonderful, creamy concoction for us. We never had powdered hot cocoa mix when I was growing up. We were farmers and we had access to all the fresh milk we could possibly need—so we had homemade hot cocoa a lot. Snowy, cold, winter days in Ohio were somehow always more enjoyable with this delightful hot drink. Those were special days. Now I love passing this same simple gift on to my own family.

3 Tbsp.	cocoa powder
½ cup	raw or white sugar
½ cup	water
5½ cups	milk (whole makes it best!)
1 Tbsp.	salted butter
⅛ tsp.	salt

Mix cocoa, sugar, and water in a medium saucepan over high heat. Heat, stirring, until sugar is dissolved. Reduce heat to low and add milk and butter. Heat just until hot, stirring frequently. Add salt. Serve. Yields 6 cups.

🍃 **And Another Thing . . . And Another Thing . . .** Serve with as many marshmallows as your mother will let you. To me that's what makes hot chocolate so good. You can also garnish with whipped cream and chocolate syrup.

Mocha Punch

6 cups	hot water
¼ cup	instant coffee
½ cup	raw or white sugar
½ cup	chocolate syrup (see recipe on page 213)
4 cups	vanilla ice cream
4 cups	chocolate ice cream
8 cups	milk

Optional:

1 cup	whipping cream
2 Tbsp.	powdered sugar
	chocolate curls
	cinnamon

In a large bowl, mix together hot water, coffee, and sugar. When sugar and coffee are completely dissolved add chocolate syrup and stir until completely mixed. Chill for 2–4 hours. To prepare punch, scoop ice cream into punch bowl, and add milk and chilled coffee mixture. Stir gently to combine. Allow to set for 15–20 minutes before serving. If desired, whip cream until soft peaks form and add powdered sugar. Serve punch with whipped cream, chocolate curls, and cinnamon. Yields 10–12 servings.

Iced Coffee

¼ cup	instant coffee
14 oz.	sweetened condensed milk
1 cup	boiling water
1 cup	cold water
1 qt.	whole milk
1 qt.	ice

Stir instant coffee and sweetened condensed milk into boiling water. Stir until dissolved. Add cold water and milk. Pour over ice. Serves 6.

🐦 **And Another Thing . . . And Another Thing . . .** I like to add 1 teaspoon vanilla to the coffee mixture for additional flavoring. This coffee looks beautiful with a dab of whipped cream and chocolate syrup drizzled on top. You can also add a quick garnish by grating a chocolate bar with a vegetable peeler.

Pina Colada Punch

2 (46 oz.) cans	pineapple juice, divided
1 (15 oz.) can	coconut milk
1 qt.	vanilla ice cream, softened
2 liters	ginger ale
	fresh pineapple wedges
	whipped cream
	shredded coconut

In blender, combine 2 cups pineapple juice with coconut milk. Stir mixture into remaining pineapple juice, ice cream, and ginger ale. Pour into glasses and garnish with a pineapple wedge slit to attach to the rim of the glass. Top with whipped cream and coconut. Yields 22 cups.

🐦 **And Another Thing . . . And Another Thing . . .** Serve this punch in pint Mason jars for an inexpensive, fun way to add some creativity.

Garden Mint Tea

Fresh garden mint tea on the farm spells SUMMER! Growing up, we drank so much of this that my parents purchased a second refrigerator just to store the tea in. I do not know where my mother found all those glass gallon containers, but when we saw the refrigerator full of that steamy drink trying to cool quickly, we always wanted that refrigerator to work extra hard. Below is a similar version of what I grew up on. This is a concentrate, so you will not need to purchase an extra refrigerator to enjoy it often. We had fuzzy mint when I was growing up, but currently I use the peppermint growing in a confined section of my garden (it will get out of control, so plant it in an area that can be contained). I like both versions of tea very much.

1½ cups	raw or white sugar
5 cups	water
3 cups	mint leaves, washed and tightly packed

Mix sugar and water in a saucepan, and heat until boiling. Remove from heat and add mint. It is very important that your mint leaves are packed tightly in your measuring cup. If they are not, your concentrate will be weak. Make sure mint is completely submerged in water. Allow the tea to steep for 6 hours, then strain. This will make a simple syrup. To serve, take 1 cup of concentrate and add 3½ cups cold water and ice. Garnish with a mint leaf and serve. Yields 6 cups concentrate.

🐦 **And Another Thing . . . And Another Thing . . .** If you find this recipe too sweet, you can reduce the amount of sugar.

Sparkling Grape Spritzer

My sister Jenelle introduced me to this recipe and it has become my all-time favorite drink to serve at a party. It accents an appetizer table beautifully and is an excellent drink to serve at a dinner party.

½ cup	raw or white sugar
1½ cups	hot water
1 (12 oz.) can	grape juice concentrate
1 (12 oz.) can	orange juice concentrate
¼ cup	lemon juice
4 liters	ginger ale

Dissolve sugar in hot water. Cool. Add grape and orange juice concentrates and lemon juice. Chill well. Just before serving, add ginger ale. Serves 8.

And Another Thing . . . And Another Thing . . . I like to garnish this drink with lemon slices and mint leaves and serve it in a large, clear glass jar as a wonderful centerpiece on a drink table at a summer party.

Food for Thought

It is the little things that make my heart flutter and help me see how the Lord romances me. Early one spring morning before my husband went to work, I wanted to run to the grocery store to take advantage of some specials that were expiring that day. It had been a particularly hard week because my boys had been feverish and grumpy all week. Then I contracted what they had in addition to having an allergy attack. As we all know, it is very difficult to mother when "Mom" is not feeling well. I had been through a rough, restless night. I threw on some rumpled clothes and departed for the grocery store. As I was leaving the store I wanted to pick up a gift card at Starbucks and, of course, sip on a cup of joe as I drove home to face my day. The sweet customer in front of me chitchatted about nothing for a bit and then went about her business, ordering a lovely latte. When she had finished I ordered my latte, and the cashier said, "Yours is paid for."

In hindsight, she might have thought I looked pitiful that morning and decided, *This dear soul can't even afford a cup of coffee, so I will just get it for her.* Or perhaps it was God speaking into my day, prompting her to bless me, and saying to me in the process, *Dawn, I see your current circumstances. I know, and I will walk with you today—and this is the way I am choosing to romance you.* I fell into God's arms and breathed deeply. Life was going to be okay. I would make it through the day. That free cup of coffee boosted my spirits. I found the lady and told her a bit about my weariness and that I would pray God would bless her in an extra special way. She responded by saying, "His blessings are greater than a thank-you."

Look for the ways God is romancing you, but also look for ways he wants you to be an instrument of his love to someone you may not even know. You never know how it may bless them, and you will experience a measure of beautiful peace in the process.

2

Breakfast and Breads

In an effort to accommodate the lifestyle of busy dairy farmers who get up early every single morning without a break, my family began the tradition of going to Mom and Dad's home every Saturday morning for brunch. I am the only child that does not live near my parents, so I miss out on this weekly adventure, but I think of them often and make it a priority to be home as often as I can for those Saturday morning meals.

This tradition was birthed during a particularly difficult time in the life of our family, and it was a way we were able to connect and process life as it was being handed to us, no matter how hard and unfair it felt. While that particular difficulty has come and gone, we still love going home every Saturday morning. Let me tell you, my mother holds nothing back. There are pancakes, eggs, Mom's special potatoes, sausage links, bacon, coffee cake, and fruit. She will also make crepes when fresh strawberries are ready in her garden, chocolate covered strawberries for Valentine's Day, or pick up cream sticks from our favorite bakery. There is something so beautiful about sitting down to a table that has been prepared and set with love.

Think about little ways you could serve your family that could become unique family traditions. I promise you it will become a gift you give your children for years to come. My mother's philosophy has always been to serve us her best, and this includes serving us off of her gorgeous stoneware dishes. She decided early in life that all who entered her home were important, but the people she lived with should feel special and loved in little ways. Don't wait until guests arrive to make your table beautiful. Surprise your family with special dinners. My mother was very intentional about this, and that has taught me such valuable lessons about truly serving my family and my guests.

Amish Breakfast Casserole

This is an all-time Falb family favorite! If you're looking for a breakfast casserole that is not very time consuming, this is it. This recipe hit the radar early in Mom's breakfast-making adventures and has remained on top. The key ingredient to this recipe is the Swiss cheese.

½ lb.	sausage
1 cup	sweet onion, chopped
6	eggs, lightly beaten
4 cups	hash browns, shredded (fresh or frozen)
2 cups	cheddar cheese, shredded
1 cup	Swiss cheese, shredded
1½ cups	small curd cottage cheese
2 Tbsp.	fresh chives, minced (or 1 Tbsp. dried)
½ tsp.	fresh cracked pepper

Preheat oven to 350°F. In a skillet, fry sausage and onion together until meat is no longer pink. Drain. In a large bowl, mix together eggs, hash browns, cheeses, cottage cheese, chives, and pepper, then stir in sausage mixture. Pour into a greased 8 x 8 pan. Bake uncovered for 45–55 minutes. Let stand 10 minutes before serving. Serves 4–6.

> 🐦 **And Another Thing . . . And Another Thing . . .** This recipe easily doubles or triples to feed larger crowds. You can also prepare this casserole the night before and place it in the refrigerator to bake in the morning. You will need to add 15 minutes to your baking time if your dish is cold when you place it in the oven.

Creamed Eggs over Toast

When I was newly married, I was on the phone one afternoon with my sister Jenelle, and I asked her what she was making for dinner. She told me about this amazing creamed egg recipe, and I made it that very night. We love it. It is a very simple dinner to prepare.

¼ cup	salted butter
¼ cup	flour
2 tsp.	prepared mustard
1 tsp.	salt
3 cups	milk
6	hard boiled eggs, peeled and diced
4 slices	bacon, cooked and crumbled
¼ lb.	American cheese
2 Tbsp.	fresh chives, minced (or 1 Tbsp. dried)
½ tsp.	fresh cracked pepper
⅛ tsp.	red pepper flakes (optional)
	toast or biscuits

Melt butter in a saucepan over medium heat. Stir in flour, mustard, and salt. Slowly add milk, stirring until smooth. Stirring constantly, cook until mixture is thickened and just starts to boil, approximately 6–8 minutes; remove from heat. Add eggs, crumbled bacon, cheese, chives, and pepper to taste. Stir until mixed. Serve over toast or biscuits. Serves 4–6.

᠀ **And Another Thing . . . And Another Thing . . .** You can make this dish 2–3 days in advance. I like having dishes like this on hand when I have guests. I am finding that the more my heart and soul are prepared for guests, and I can relax instead of frantically flying around the house, the more I enjoy my guests. I like to serve good food, but I don't like to spend the whole day in the kitchen because it makes me weary. Dishes like this are ways I have found to simplify my life and enjoy the people God brings into my path.

Farmer's Skillet

1 lb.	pork sausage
2½ cups	red potatoes, cubed
1	red bell pepper, diced
1	green bell pepper, diced
4	green onions, chopped (or ½ cup onion, diced)
1	garlic clove, minced
6–7	eggs, lightly beaten
½ tsp.	salt
½ tsp.	fresh cracked pepper
½ tsp.	paprika
2 tsp.	dried chives (or 1 Tbsp. fresh)
2 Tbsp.	fresh parsley, minced (or 1 Tbsp. dried)
1 cup	cheddar cheese, shredded
	additional parsley (to garnish)

In a large skillet over medium heat, cook sausage and potatoes until potatoes are soft, about 8–10 minutes. Drain most of the drippings from skillet. Return skillet to heat and add peppers, onions, and garlic. Cook for 5 minutes, stirring frequently. Lightly beat eggs with salt, pepper, paprika, chives, and parsley. Pour egg mixture into skillet and reduce heat to low; cover and cook until eggs are set. Sprinkle cheese on top. Garnish with additional parsley. Serves 6.

Fluffy Baked Eggs

My mother-in-law raised eleven children and made baked eggs often. This recipe is a tribute to her and the many meals she cooked to feed her large family.

2 Tbsp.	salted butter
4 oz.	cream cheese, softened
8	eggs
½ cup	whipping cream
¼ cup	onion, chopped
½ tsp.	salt
¼ tsp.	cracked black pepper
½ cup	cheddar cheese, shredded
1 Tbsp.	dried chives
1 Tbsp.	dried parsley

Preheat oven to 350°F. Melt butter in an 8 x 8 baking dish. Beat cream cheese until fluffy. In another bowl, whisk eggs well. Add cream cheese, whipping cream, onion, salt, pepper, cheddar cheese, chives, and parsley. Pour into baking dish. Bake for 35–40 minutes or until set. These get puffy while they bake.

And Another Thing . . . And Another Thing . . . This is a great recipe to get creative with. You can take this basic recipe and make it as simple or as gourmet as you like. Add 1 cup diced ham, 1 cup cooked and crumbled bacon, ½ cup diced green or red pepper, or ½ cup diced mushrooms. You can also mix this up the night before and place it in the refrigerator. All you have to do in the morning is pull it out and bake it. You will need to add 10–15 minutes to your baking time.

Sausage and Cheese Omelet Roll

4 oz.	cream cheese, softened
¾ cup	milk
2 Tbsp.	flour
1 Tbsp.	dried chives
½ tsp.	salt
¼ tsp.	fresh cracked pepper
12	eggs
1 lb.	sausage
½ cup	onion, chopped
½ cup	green bell pepper, chopped
½ cup	mushrooms, diced
2	garlic cloves, diced
2½ cups	cheese, shredded and divided (cheddar and Swiss make an excellent combo)
¼ cup	green onions, thinly sliced

Preheat oven to 375°F. Line the bottom and sides of a 10 x 15 jelly roll pan with tinfoil. Grease the tinfoil with butter or cooking spray. *This step is very important.*

In a small bowl, beat the cream cheese until smooth; add milk, flour, chives, salt, and pepper. Stir until combined. In a large mixing bowl, beat the eggs until blended and fluffy (at least 3 minutes). Add cream cheese mixture and stir well. Pour into prepared pan. Bake for 25 minutes or until eggs are set and puffy.

In a skillet, fully cook sausage, onion, green pepper, mushrooms, and garlic. Cover with a lid to keep hot until ready to use.

Remove eggs from oven and immediately sprinkle with 1 cup cheese. Then sprinkle sausage mixture, green onions, and 1 more cup of cheese on top. Roll up from the long side, carefully removing the foil as you roll. Place on baking sheet and sprinkle with remaining ½ cup cheese. Bake an additional 4–5 minutes and remove from oven. Slice and serve. You may garnish with additional green onions and chopped tomatoes. Serves 8.

Sausage Cranberry Mini Quiches

½ lb.	sausage
½ cup	onion, chopped
½ cup	green bell pepper, chopped
2 (8 oz.) tubes	crescent rolls
4	eggs
1½ cups	half-and-half
1 Tbsp.	fresh parsley (or 1½ tsp. dried)
½ tsp.	salt
¼ tsp.	fresh cracked pepper
¾ cup	dried cranberries
1½ cups	Monterey Jack or cheddar cheese, shredded

Preheat oven to 350°F. In a large skillet, cook sausage, onion, and green pepper until sausage is no longer pink. While this is cooking, unroll crescent rolls and flatten them, then press each roll into one cup of a well-greased muffin tin. Seal edges well so there are no holes for the egg mixture to escape.

Beat eggs; add half-and-half, parsley, salt, and pepper. Stir in cranberries, cheese, and sausage mixture. Using a ¼-cup measure, scoop egg mixture into muffin wells. Do not overfill.

Bake for 35–40 minutes or until egg mixture is set. Allow to sit for 5 minutes before removing from muffin pans. Yields 16 quiches.

Swiss Cheese Quiche

This dish was inspired by the streets of France. I was sitting at a streetside café with my friends Rita and Sheree, eating quiche and fresh salad and drinking a good cup of coffee, and a star was born. The possibilities are endless in creating your own signature quiche. Go ahead and be creative.

1 Tbsp.	olive oil
½ cup	onion, chopped
½ cup	green bell pepper, chopped
½ cup	fresh mushrooms, sliced
4	eggs
1¼ cups	half-and-half
½ tsp.	salt
¼ tsp.	fresh cracked pepper
1 Tbsp.	fresh parsley, chopped (or 1½ tsp. dried)
1 Tbsp.	fresh chives, chopped (or 1½ tsp. dried)
1 Tbsp.	flour
2 cups	Swiss cheese, shredded
½ lb.	bacon slices, cooked and crumbled (or ¾ cup ham, diced)
1 cup	fresh spinach, chopped (optional)
1	unbaked deep dish piecrust

Preheat oven to 350°F. Sauté onion and green pepper for 3–4 minutes in olive oil. Add mushrooms and cook for 2 more minutes. Remove from heat. Combine eggs, half-and-half, salt, pepper, parsley, chives, and flour. Mix well. Add Swiss cheese, bacon, and sautéed vegetables to the egg mixture. Stir in spinach, if using. Pour into unbaked piecrust. Bake for 45–55 minutes or until golden on top. Remove from oven and let stand for 10 minutes before slicing. Serves 6.

And Another Thing . . . And Another Thing . . . I like to place the quiche on a cookie sheet lined with foil just in case the egg mixture runs over. Another helpful cleaning tip is when baking bacon, line your cookie sheet with foil. When the bacon is cooled, you can pull the tinfoil up and throw the mess in the garbage, leaving your cookie sheet barely dirty. If you are hosting a brunch and prefer to do mini-quiches, make half of the quiche filling recipe and instead of using a piecrust, unroll a tube of crescent rolls and press each roll into a greased, oversized muffin pan. Pour the egg mixture into each cup. Do not overfill, or you will have a nasty, burnt smell as your guests arrive. I have had that happen to me! Sprinkle with chives or parsley and bake for 30–35 minutes. Yields 8 mini quiches. They are so fun to serve individually on a plate with an assortment of fruit. We ladies love little touches like this.

Granola with Flax Seed

8 cups	oatmeal (I prefer old fashioned)
2 cups	flaked coconut
2 cups	wheat germ
1 cup	whole flax seed
2 cups	brown sugar
2 cups	pecans or walnuts, chopped
3 Tbsp.	cinnamon
1 cup	salted butter

Preheat oven to 300°F. Mix oatmeal, coconut, wheat germ, flax seed, brown sugar, pecans, and cinnamon together. Melt butter and pour over mixture. Toss to coat evenly and spread onto 2 cookie sheets. Bake for 1 hour, stirring every 20 minutes. Yields 34 ½-cup servings.

Baked Oatmeal with Apples and Pecans

This recipe tastes like an oatmeal cookie—and the best part is you get to eat it for breakfast with a little bit of milk and call it cereal.

¼ cup	olive oil or melted butter
½ cup + 1 Tbsp.	brown sugar, divided
2	eggs
1 Tbsp.	vanilla extract
½ tsp.	salt
1 tsp.	cinnamon
1 tsp.	baking powder
1 cup	milk
2½ cups	oatmeal (I prefer old fashioned)
2 Tbsp.	flax seed (optional)
2 cups	apples, peeled and diced (any apple will work)
½ cup	golden raisins or dried cranberries
½ cup	pecan pieces
2 Tbsp.	salted butter

Preheat oven to 350°F. Spray an 8 x 8 baking pan with nonstick cooking spray. In a bowl, cream together oil, ½ cup brown sugar, eggs, vanilla, salt, and cinnamon. Add baking powder, milk, and oats. Stir until oats are well moistened. Stir in flax seed, apples, raisins or cranberries, and pecans. Pour into prepared pan. Dot with butter and sprinkle with remaining 1 tablespoon brown sugar. Bake uncovered for 30 minutes until lightly browned. This may be served with or without milk. Serves 6. This is an excellent recipe to make the night before and put in the refrigerator. You will need to increase the baking time by 20–30 minutes.

&❧ **And Another Thing . . . And Another Thing . . .** If you want to use a 9 x 13 baking dish, double the recipe and add 10 minutes to the baking time. Also, I like to add oat or wheat germ to this recipe to give it some extra nutritional value. To do that I reduce the oatmeal to 2 ¼ cups and add ¼ cup of germ.

Peanut Butter Granola

3 cups	rolled oats
½ cup	dry roasted peanuts
½ cup	flaked coconut
¼ cup	wheat bran or germ
¼ cup	whole flax seed
½ cup	peanut butter
½ cup	brown sugar, firmly packed
¼ cup	salted butter
2 Tbsp.	honey
¼ tsp.	salt

Preheat oven to 350°F. Toss together oats, peanuts, coconut, wheat bran or germ, and flax seed.

In a small saucepan, heat peanut butter, brown sugar, butter, honey, and salt for 3 minutes over medium heat. Remove from heat and pour over oat mixture. Toss to coat. Spread mixture evenly on a lightly greased jelly roll pan. Bake for 15–20 minutes or until lightly browned, stirring every 10 minutes. Yields 5 cups.

🐦 **And Another Thing . . . And Another Thing . . .** I like to double this recipe because if I am going to the bother of getting my kitchen messy, why not make a larger batch? It freezes well!

Dad's French Toast

While my father's strengths shine in the farmyard and not so much in the kitchen, this dish is his specialty. We all loved French toast days. I think the only other thing I remember my father making was fried eggs. This was our "snowy day" treat from him. As a grown daughter I now really appreciate the gift he gave us in the form of this dish. You see, it's not so much what we ate, but that he made it for us with love. And while everyone in the kitchen might have been frazzled when he was trying to make the French toast, the one thing we never let him forget was the powdered sugar sprinkled on top!

2	eggs, slightly beaten
½ cup	milk
¼ tsp.	salt
1 tsp.	raw or white sugar
½ tsp.	cinnamon
½ tsp.	vanilla extract
2 Tbsp.	salted butter, divided
6 slices	bread
	powdered sugar

Mix together eggs, milk, salt, sugar, cinnamon, and vanilla. Heat 1–2 teaspoons of butter in a frying pan or griddle over medium-high heat. Dip each piece of bread into the egg mixture, just until moist, and transfer to a hot frying pan. Fry on each side until golden brown. Add more butter as needed. Sprinkle with powdered sugar and serve immediately. Serves 4.

🐓 **And Another Thing . . . And Another Thing . . .** Wait to add the butter until griddle is very hot. This will give your French toast crispy edges but bread that is light, fluffy, and spongy. Pure maple syrup takes this family recipe to another level of goodness!

Baked Peach French Toast

4 oz.	cream cheese, softened
10 slices	bread
3	fresh peaches, peeled and sliced (or 29 oz. canned peach slices, drained)
½ cup	pecans, chopped
3	eggs
1 cup	milk
⅓ cup	maple syrup or pancake syrup
2 Tbsp.	salted butter, melted
1 Tbsp.	raw or white sugar
2 tsp.	cinnamon
1 tsp.	vanilla extract

Preheat oven to 400°F. Spread cream cheese on one side of each bread slice. Place the pieces of bread, cream cheese side up, in a greased 9 x 13 baking dish, overlapping slightly. Top with peach slices and sprinkle with pecans. In a large bowl, whisk together eggs, milk, syrup, butter, sugar, cinnamon, and vanilla. Pour mixture over bread and bake for 25–35 minutes or until set in center. Serves 6–8.

Cream Cheese Spreads for Bagels

Sometimes I feel tension to create a big, elaborate brunch for the guests I have invited over. Tension can be good, but it can also cause us to not invite someone over when we should. I have found these simple spreads to be so delicious to serve. Make a couple of varieties and serve them with mini bagels, and you'll have created a very nice breakfast entrée without a lot of stress—and without a lot of last-minute work, because you can make these spreads days ahead of your event!

Chocolate Raspberry Cream Cheese Spread

8 oz.	cream cheese, softened
3 Tbsp.	powdered sugar
½ cup	frozen red raspberries, thawed and drained
¼ cup	mini chocolate chips

Beat cream cheese until smooth and creamy. Add powdered sugar and stir. Gently fold in raspberries and chocolate chips. Serve.

Cinnamon Apple Cream Cheese Spread

8 oz.	cream cheese, softened
2 Tbsp.	brown sugar
1½ tsp.	cinnamon
1 small	apple, peeled and chopped fine

Beat cream cheese until smooth and creamy. Add brown sugar and cinnamon. Stir well. Add diced apple. Serve.

Feta, Cranberry, and Walnut Cream Cheese Spread

8 oz.	cream cheese, softened
½ cup	dried cranberries
¼ cup	feta cheese
¼ cup	walnuts, chopped
⅛ tsp.	fresh cracked pepper

Beat cream cheese until smooth and creamy. Add remaining ingredients. Stir well. Serve.

Savory Herb Cream Cheese Spread

8 oz.	cream cheese, softened
½ cup	cheddar cheese, shredded
¼ cup	ham or cooked bacon, crumbled
1 Tbsp.	onion, diced
1 tsp.	dried chives
1 tsp.	dried basil
1 tsp.	dried parsley
⅛ tsp.	fresh cracked pepper

Beat cream cheese until smooth and creamy. Add remaining ingredients. Stir well. Serve.

Raspberry Cream Cheese Squares

I find that breakfast can sometimes be hard to accomplish in a simple fashion, especially with two little boys tugging at my feet. It's particularly difficult when there are guests in our home. I want to serve them something delicious—without waking up before the chickens. This is a quick breakfast treat that will be sure to satisfy the sweet palate.

2 (8 oz.) cans	refrigerated crescent rolls
16 oz.	cream cheese, softened
1 tsp.	almond or vanilla extract
2	eggs
1 cup	raw or white sugar, divided
2 cups	red raspberries or blueberries

Icing:

½ cup	powdered sugar
4 tsp.	milk

Preheat oven to 350°F. Unroll 1 can of crescent rolls. Press onto the bottom of a greased 9 x 13 baking pan. Firmly press seams together to seal.

Beat cream cheese, extract, eggs, and ¾ cup sugar until well blended. Spread onto crust. Sprinkle berries on top of cream cheese mixture. Unroll remaining crescent rolls onto a piece of wax paper. Pat out dough to firmly press seams together. Invert dough over filling to form a top crust. Remove wax paper and sprinkle remaining ¼ cup of sugar on top of dough. Bake for 35–40 minutes until golden. Cut into squares. Mix powdered sugar and milk together and drizzle on top of squares. Yields 20 squares.

Croissant Sandwiches with Fresh Berries

I only vaguely remember the details of an overnight junior high school function in Columbus, Ohio, but I do remember that our gracious host served us a version of these. I remember the little vow I made to myself that day that when I was "all grown up and mature and hosting guests" I would serve these.

They are amazingly simple, but charming. I enjoy dreaming (a lot actually), and someday if my dream of a bed and breakfast takes wing, this will be on the menu. These are very filling and delicious. Serve on a nice salad plate with a mint sprig, and your guests will feel loved!

1 cup	fresh blueberries
2 cups	fresh strawberries, hulled and sliced
2	bananas, sliced
1 cup	whipping cream
½ cup	powdered sugar
8 oz.	cream cheese, softened
½ cup	raspberry yogurt
8	croissants

Wash blueberries and strawberries and set aside to dry. Beat whipping cream until soft peaks form, and add powdered sugar. In another bowl, beat cream cheese until light and fluffy; stir in yogurt and whipped cream. Slice croissants horizontally and spread ¼ cup of cream cheese mixture on bottom half of each croissant. Layer with bananas, strawberries, and blueberries. Place top half on each croissant to form a sandwich. Sprinkle additional powdered sugar on top. Eat with a knife and fork because they are messy, but oh so good! Yields 8.

🍃 **And Another Thing . . . And Another Thing . . .** It does not work to just add the cream cheese to the whipping cream. The cream cheese will be lumpy—you must beat these separately.

Crepes

Crepes will always remind me of those wonderful days gone by when my friends and I tromped around in France. We would buy from street vendors these delicious warm crepes filled with Nutella (found near the peanut butter at your local supermarket). I can still taste that warm, melting chocolate hazelnut spread. It would run everywhere and make me look like I was a kid again.

1 cup	flour
1 Tbsp.	sugar
1½ cups	milk
2	eggs, lightly beaten
½ tsp.	vanilla extract
pinch	salt

In a mixing bowl, combine all ingredients. Stir well. Cover and refrigerate for 1 hour (you may eliminate this step if you are in a hurry). In a greased skillet over medium heat, pour ¼ cup of batter. Lift and tilt pan to evenly coat bottom of pan with crepe mixture. The thinner the mixture is in the pan, the easier it will be to fold the crepe. Cook until top appears dry, about 2–3 minutes; turn and cook 15 seconds longer. Remove from heat and place on wire rack. Serve warm with Fresh Berry Filling or Nutella and Banana Filling. Yields 18 crepes. To store, place paper towel between each crepe. You can store extras in the freezer for 1–2 months.

Fresh Berry Filling

3 cups	strawberries, hulled and sliced (or try combining blackberries and red raspberries)
2 cups	vanilla yogurt
½ cup	powdered sugar
1 Tbsp.	lime juice
1½ tsp.	lime zest
⅛ tsp.	salt

Combine berries in a small bowl. In a separate bowl, combine yogurt, powdered sugar, lime juice, lime zest, and salt. Spread 2 tablespoons of yogurt mixture over each crepe; top with ⅓ cup of berries. Roll up; drizzle with 1 tablespoon yogurt mixture and top with a few berries and additional lime zest. Yields 10 crepes.

Nutella and Banana Filling

    2 Tbsp. Nutella
    ½ banana, sliced

Spread Nutella on a crepe and add banana slices. Roll up and serve.

Fresh Fruit with Lime Ginger Syrup

Syrup:
    ⅓ cup fresh lime juice
    ⅓ cup water
    ⅓ cup orange juice
    2 Tbsp. sugar
    2 Tbsp. honey
    ¼ tsp. fresh ginger, grated
    ½ tsp. lime zest
    ½ tsp. orange zest

Suggested fruit variety:
    1½ cups fresh pineapple, cubed
    1½ cups fresh strawberries, sliced
    3 kiwis, diced
    1 cup blueberries (fresh or frozen)
    1 (11 oz.) can mandarin oranges, drained

For syrup, combine first 6 ingredients in a small saucepan and bring to a boil over medium heat; cook for 5 minutes, stirring constantly. Remove from heat; add lime and orange zest. Combine fruit in a bowl. Pour ⅓ cup syrup over fruit and gently toss. Cover and chill for 1 hour (you can eliminate this step if you are in a hurry). This recipe yields 1 cup of glaze, and I use ⅓ cup to every 6 cups of fruit. You can use whatever fruit you choose, so go ahead and mix it up.

Frozen Creamy Cups

These are delightful served with quiche!

2 cups	whipping cream
1 cup	powdered sugar
8 oz.	cream cheese, softened
¼ cup	raw or white sugar
1½ cups	frozen raspberries, thawed and drained
2	bananas, sliced into bite-size pieces
1 (20 oz.) can	crushed pineapple, drained

Beat whipping cream until soft peaks form; add powdered sugar and beat until stiff peaks form, then set aside. In a separate bowl, beat cream cheese well and then add sugar. Mix in thawed raspberries. Fold in bananas, pineapple, and whipped cream. Freeze in individual 8 oz. clear plastic cups for 8–10 hours. Arrange by each place setting for an attractive side at a brunch. Allow to sit at room temperature at least 15 minutes before serving.

🐦 **And Another Thing . . . And Another Thing . . .** If you don't want to do individual cups, you can also freeze this in a 9 x 13 pan or a pretty dish. Also, you can use strawberries in place of raspberries, but I really prefer the raspberries. They give it such a rich taste. While the recipe calls to serve this dish frozen, I love it frozen or thawed.

Homemade Yogurt

I have a dear, sweet friend named Amber who has known financial hardship. Recently, it had been three months since she had seen the inside of a grocery store. Her story speaks to me. She has shown me how it is possible to live with less and be creative with your resources. In the months when things were really hard, she would make four gallons of this recipe each week to feed her five precious children. The milk would come from her parents' farm, and it became their primary source of nutrition. She shared this recipe with our ladies' group and many of us fell in love with its simplicity and the minimal cost.

½ gallon   milk
¼ cup   plain Greek yogurt with live cultures
candy thermometer

Pour milk into a large, heavy stockpot. Place a candy thermometer in the pan. Over medium heat, cook until milk reaches 180°F, stirring occasionally. Do not allow milk to scorch. When it reaches 180°F, remove from heat and immediately set stockpot into a sink of cold ice water and cool to 110°F. (Amber suggests removing it from the sink at 112°F.) Add Greek yogurt, stirring very well and making sure your culture is completely dissolved.

Pour yogurt into 2 clean quart jars. Cover with lids and place jars into an ice chest that has been filled with 2–3 inches of warm water. Set jars in the ice chest for approximately 6 hours. If it does not set to your liking, allow it to set 2 more hours. Note: the longer you allow it to sit in the water bath, the stronger the yogurt gets. If you prefer a mild flavor, remove it promptly at 6 hours.

🐚 **And Another Thing . . . And Another Thing . . .** Amber suggests sweetening 1 quart of yogurt with 3 tablespoons sugar and 1 tablespoon vanilla, or you can sweeten it with honey. You can also make frozen yogurt; add ½ cup sugar and 1 cup berries to 1 quart of yogurt and place in an ice cream freezer and follow manufacturer's instructions. Amber will also use this plain yogurt in place of mayonnaise, sour cream, and oil or shortening in baking recipes. Yogurt has great health benefits, so this is a great way to reduce extra fat in some recipes.

Homemade Vanilla Yogurt

I think you get a different flavor when you add sugar directly to the cooking process, as in this recipe.

1 Tbsp.	unflavored gelatin (I use Knox)
⅓ cup	cold water
2 qts.	milk
½ cup	raw or white sugar
1 Tbsp.	vanilla extract (or 2 tsp. vanilla bean seeds)
2 Tbsp.	plain Greek yogurt with live cultures
	candy thermometer

Dissolve gelatin in water and mix thoroughly. Heat milk in a heavy saucepan on medium heat, stirring occasionally to prevent scorching, until milk reaches 190°F. Add gelatin, sugar, and vanilla. Stir completely. Remove from heat and allow to cool to 130°F. Add Greek yogurt and whisk into the yogurt completely (this step is really important). Pour into 2 clean quart jars and screw on lids. Set in cold oven with only the oven light on for 8 hours. Chill and enjoy. Add fruit if you would like!

🐦 **And Another Thing . . . And Another Thing . . .** This is such a great way to use up milk that is just about to go bad. I enjoy using this recipe to make drinkable yogurt.

French Puff Cinnamon Muffins

These melt in your mouth. They're like donuts—without being fried. And so simple to make! Yeah!

½ cup	white or raw sugar
¼ cup	salted butter, softened
¾ tsp.	cinnamon
½ cup	milk
1 tsp.	baking powder
1 cup	flour

Cinnamon mixture:

¼ cup	salted butter
½ cup	white or raw sugar
1 tsp.	cinnamon

Preheat oven to 375°F. Grease 24 mini muffin cups. Mix sugar, butter, and cinnamon in a bowl. Stir in milk, and then mix in baking powder and flour until combined. Do not overmix. Fill prepared mini muffin cups about half full and bake until lightly golden, 15–20 minutes.

While muffins are baking, prepare the cinnamon mixture by melting butter. In a separate bowl, mix together sugar and cinnamon. When muffins are done, let cool slightly and remove from their cups, then dip each muffin completely in melted butter and roll in sugar-cinnamon mixture. Yields 18–20 mini muffins. Serve warm!

🐄 **And Another Thing . . . And Another Thing . . .** The key is to put these in a mini muffin pan. They are such a fun food and when you bake them in a mini muffin pan you can eat more without feeling guilty.

Blueberry Cream Muffins

The less stirring you do to a muffin batter, the more moist, crumbly, sweet, and delicious the muffin will turn out. You want it to melt as it touches your lips. It will be like a little party in your mouth. These turn out golden on top and soft on the inside.

½ cup	salted butter, softened
⅔ cup	raw or white sugar
½ cup	plain yogurt or sour cream
1	egg
½ tsp.	almond extract
½ tsp.	vanilla extract
2 tsp.	baking soda
½ tsp.	salt
2¼ cups	cake flour
1 cup	half-and-half
1½ cups	blueberries (frozen work great)

Glaze:

½ cup	powdered sugar
1½ Tbsp.	milk

Preheat oven to 350°F. In a large bowl, mix butter and sugar until well blended. Add yogurt, egg, and extracts. Stir in the baking soda, salt, flour, and half-and-half. Beat just until mixed. Add blueberries. Stir just until combined. Fill greased baking cups and bake for 18–22 minutes or until toothpick inserted in center comes out clean. While muffins cool, mix powdered sugar and milk together. Drizzle over muffins. Yields 12–14 muffins.

🐦 **And Another Thing . . . And Another Thing . . .** If you don't have cake flour on hand or you don't want to purchase it, here is an inexpensive way to make it: place 2 tablespoons cornstarch in a 1 cup measuring cup, then fill the cup with all-purpose flour. So, for this recipe, you would need 2 cups all-purpose flour and ¼ cup cornstarch.

Lemon Raspberry Crumb Muffins

2 cups	raw or white sugar
4	eggs
1 cup	plain yogurt or sour cream
1 cup	salted butter, softened
2 Tbsp.	lemon juice
	zest of 2 lemons
3 cups	cake flour (or 1 cup cake flour and 2 cups white wheat flour)
1 tsp.	baking soda
½ tsp.	salt
2 cups	red raspberries, frozen

Streusel:

½ cup	flour
½ cup	sugar
2 Tbsp.	salted butter, softened

Lemon glaze:

½ cup	powdered sugar
1 Tbsp.	lemon juice
	lemon zest for garnish (optional)

Preheat oven to 350°F. Beat sugar and eggs until light and fluffy, then add yogurt, butter, and lemon juice; beat until mixed together. Fold in lemon zest. Add flour, baking soda, and salt. Blend just until well mixed; do not overmix. Fold in raspberries. Place in muffin pan.

For streusel, mix ingredients together to form a crumbly mixture. Sprinkle 1 generous tablespoon on top of each muffin. Bake for 20–25 minutes or until toothpick inserted in center comes out clean. For glaze, stir together powdered sugar and lemon juice until smooth. Poke holes in tops of warm muffins with a fork. Drizzle glaze over top of muffins. Garnish with lemon zest if desired. Allow to sit for 15 minutes before removing from pan. Yields 2 dozen muffins.

🐦 **And Another Thing . . . And Another Thing . . .** If you do not have a zester, you can use a vegetable peeler. Be sure to make small, short strokes so you don't get long pieces of rind.

Pecan Pear Muffins

I love to be in my friend Rita's home. She truly has the gift of hospitality. She will randomly call me up and invite me over for muffins and coffee. Those are fun mornings! But it's so much more than "fun" mornings. We are learning to live in community. She is my neighbor and she is my friend.

2	eggs
1 cup	canola oil
1¾ cups	raw or white sugar
1 tsp.	vanilla
3 cups	all-purpose flour
2 tsp.	baking powder
1 tsp.	cinnamon
½ tsp.	salt
4 cups	pears, peeled and chopped
1 cup	pecans, finely chopped

Preheat oven to 350°F. Mix together eggs and oil, then add sugar and vanilla. Mix well. Add flour, baking powder, cinnamon, and salt. Stir just until moistened. Fold in pears and pecans. Fill paper-lined muffin cups two thirds full. Bake for 20–25 minutes or until toothpick inserted in center comes out clean. Cool for 5 minutes, then remove from pans to wire racks. Yields 2 dozen.

&⬥ **And Another Thing . . . And Another Thing . . .** For these muffins you can replace half of the all-purpose flour with white wheat flour, if desired.

Maple Almond Muffins

Ohio, my home state, is known for its pure maple syrup; however, I did not grow up on pure maple syrup, partly due to the sticker price. But now that I understand how true maple syrup possesses some healthy trace minerals, I keep it on hand. I have good friends whose grandmother owns a sugar house, and they still tap the maple trees and cook down the sap. It is such a process! It takes 40 gallons of sap to produce 1 gallon of maple syrup. It was these friends who introduced me to the love of all things maple. We sold maple cookies at The Farmer's Wife, and sometimes I would allow myself two—and no more than two because I would have eaten the whole package—maple cookies with a cup of fresh brewed coffee for my late afternoon snack. Yum! Maple lattes, pure maple syrup on pancakes, or maple candy—any of these will do when it's cold and snowy outside.

½ cup	plain yogurt
¼ cup	olive oil
2	eggs
1 cup	milk
1 cup	pure maple syrup
1½ cups	white wheat flour
1½ cups	all-purpose flour (if you don't want to use white wheat flour just use 3¼ cups all-purpose)
½ cup	granola cereal
1 Tbsp.	baking powder

Maple icing:

8 oz.	cream cheese
½ cup	powdered sugar
¼ cup	pure maple syrup
2 Tbsp.	slivered almonds

Preheat oven to 375°F. Cream together yogurt, oil, and eggs. Add milk and maple syrup. Mix both flours, granola, and baking powder together. Add to creamed mixture. Stir just until moistened. Batter will be a little lumpy. Pour into greased muffin tins and bake for 15 minutes or until toothpick inserted in center comes out clean. For icing, beat cream cheese until smooth. Add powdered sugar and maple syrup and beat some more. Frost cooled muffins with a thin layer of icing and sprinkle slivered almonds on top. Yields 12–15 muffins.

Pumpkin Cinnamon Rolls

To me, fall just spells pumpkin and cinnamon! This is a particularly delightful treat to serve when the leaves are falling and the wind has a chill to it.

⅔ cup	milk
¼ cup	salted butter
1 cup	pumpkin purée
¼ cup	brown sugar
1 tsp.	salt
2	eggs, beaten
2 Tbsp.	yeast
4 cups	bread flour

Cinnamon mixture:

¼ cup	salted butter, melted
⅔ cup	brown sugar
3 Tbsp.	cinnamon

Cream cheese glaze:

8 oz.	cream cheese
2 cups	powdered sugar
2 Tbsp.	half-and-half or milk
½ tsp.	vanilla extract
pinch	salt

In a saucepan, heat milk and butter until butter is almost melted, then remove from heat and set aside. In a mixing bowl, combine pumpkin, sugar, salt, and milk mixture. Beat well. Add beaten eggs, yeast, and ½ cup flour. Beat on low for 2 minutes. Add remaining flour and mix well. Knead dough for 5 minutes. Dough will be soft. Place into a greased bowl, turning once to grease all sides of dough, and cover. Let rise for 1 hour. Punch dough down and roll out into a rectangle on a floured surface.

For cinnamon mixture, melt butter and spread with your hand evenly over the dough. Combine brown sugar and cinnamon and sprinkle over butter. Roll up from the long side and cut into 1-inch pieces. Place in a greased 9 x 13 pan. Let rise for 30–40 minutes. Preheat oven to 350°F and bake for 18–20 minutes. For the glaze, beat cream cheese until smooth. Add powdered sugar, half-and-half, vanilla, and salt. Beat together and spread on warm rolls. Don't you just wish these rolls would make themselves? Yields 10–12 servings.

And Another Thing . . . And Another Thing . . . The biggest challenge I had to overcome with yeast recipes was having enough patience. If my dough had not risen in the mentioned time, I thought I had killed my yeast. I would get terribly impatient. But I just needed to learn to wait until the dough really is double in size. It might take longer than the recipe says, depending on the weather and the temperature of your kitchen.

Cinnamon Rolls

There is something about cinnamon rolls that communicate love to me. Maybe it's the knowledge that someone went to the bother of making sweet yeast dough, waited the time it takes to allow it to rise completely, and then lovingly rolled it out and added some yummy cinnamon and sugar. I think the key to this recipe is the potato flakes, which keep the dough soft. I tend to get impatient as I wait for these to rise, but it is so important to let the yeast do its work. It is well worth the wait!

2 Tbsp.	yeast
1 tsp.	raw or white sugar
½ cup	lukewarm water
½ cup	salted butter, softened
½ cup	raw or white sugar
2	eggs
2 tsp.	salt
1½ cups	lukewarm milk
½ cup	potato flakes
3 cups	bread flour
1½–2 cups	white wheat flour

Cinnamon sugar mixture:

½ cup	salted butter, melted
1 cup	brown sugar
2 Tbsp.	cinnamon

In a small bowl, dissolve yeast and 1 teaspoon sugar in warm water. In a large mixing bowl, beat together butter, sugar, eggs, and salt. Add yeast mixture and warm milk; mix together. Add potato flakes and 4 cups of flour and beat until smooth. Mix in enough remaining flour to make a very moist but easy to handle dough. The stickier the dough the better your cinnamon rolls will be, but it also makes it harder to roll them out when they are too sticky.

Turn dough onto lightly floured surface and knead until dough is smooth and elastic, about 5 minutes. Place in a lightly oiled bowl. Turn once to oil all sides of dough. Cover and let rise in a warm place until double in size, about 1 hour.

Divide dough in half; roll one half out into a very thin rectangle. Spread with ¼ cup butter. Combine brown sugar and cinnamon; sprinkle half of the mixture evenly over butter. Roll up tightly, beginning at the wide end. Cut into 1-inch slices and place rolls in a greased 9 x 13 pan. Repeat with remaining half of dough, butter, and sugar cinnamon mixture. Cover and let rise until double in size, 60–90 minutes. Bake at 350°F for 15–17 minutes or until lightly golden.

Frost with Brown Sugar Frosting II (page 203) or Cream Cheese Frosting (page 203).

🐌 **And Another Thing . . . And Another Thing . . .** You can use 5–5½ cups of all-purpose flour, but I personally like to use bread flour because I think it helps to make a softer dough. I also like to use wheat flour so that there is some nutritional benefit to this yummy breakfast treat. An easy trick to cut the rolled-up dough: dental floss! Bring floss beneath the roll of dough, then pull upward and crisscross. It makes a nice clean cut and doesn't squish the cinnamon roll.

A variation to this recipe is Raspberry Rolls. Replace the butter, cinnamon, and sugar with raspberry pie filling; all other steps are the same. Raspberry Rolls are divine with Cream Cheese Frosting (page 203). They make a great item for Christmas morning breakfast or a brunch. Another variation is a fall flavor, adding minced apples, brown sugar, and cinnamon instead of sugar. Frost these with Brown Sugar Frosting II (page 203).

Fresh Apple Walnut Bread with Maple Drizzle

What is it about fresh baked apples that creates this warm, cozy feeling for me? This recipe is no exception, especially because this is a healthier approach to apple bread, and replaces half of the oil with yogurt. It feels good to be giving my family a healthy choice. This makes an excellent breakfast bread!

1 cup	raw sugar (or ½ cup white plus ½ cup brown)
¾ cup	plain yogurt or sour cream
¾ cup	canola oil
2	eggs
2 tsp.	vanilla extract
1¾ cups	white wheat flour (or 2 cups all-purpose flour)
2 tsp.	baking powder
½ tsp.	baking soda
½ tsp.	salt
1½ cups	apples, peeled and chopped
1 cup	walnuts, chopped
¼ cup	salted butter
2 Tbsp.	brown sugar
2 Tbsp.	pure maple syrup

Preheat oven to 350°F. In a large mixing bowl, beat together sugar, yogurt, oil, eggs, and vanilla until well mixed. Add flour, baking powder, baking soda, and salt. Beat just until combined. Stir in apples and nuts. Pour into a greased loaf pan or small Bundt pan. Bake for 45–55 minutes or until toothpick inserted in center comes out clean. Cool on rack for 10 minutes before turning loaf out of pan.

In a saucepan, combine butter, brown sugar, and maple syrup. Cook and stir until mixture comes to a boil; reduce heat. Boil for 1 minute. Drizzle bread with syrup. So yummy served warm! Yields 1½ lb. loaf (12–14 slices), or you can bake it in 2 small loaf pans.

Honey Corn Bread

This is a great side to serve with chili or vegetable soup and, oh, so simple to make!

⅓ cup	salted butter, softened
⅓ cup	raw or white sugar
½ cup	honey
4	eggs
1⅓ cups	milk
2⅓ cups	flour
1½ Tbsp.	baking powder
½ cup	cornmeal
1 tsp.	salt

Preheat oven to 350°F. Cream butter, sugar, and honey; add eggs and beat well. Add milk, flour, baking powder, cornmeal, and salt just until combined. Do not overmix. Batter will be lumpy. Pour into a greased 9 x 9 baking dish. Bake for 15–20 minutes or until knife inserted in center comes out clean. Yields 9 squares.

🐦 **And Another Thing . . . And Another Thing . . .** An easy way to have honey release from a measuring cup is to spray the measuring cup with cooking spray before adding honey. The honey will pour out without a mess.

Garlic Herb Braid

There is nothing like the aroma of fresh bread baking to warm your heart and home on any given day. If you are looking for a nice, crusty European-style bread, this is it.

¾ cup	milk
¼ cup	salted butter
2 Tbsp.	yeast
3 Tbsp.	sugar
½ cup	warm water
2 cups	bread flour
1¾–2 cups	white wheat flour
2 tsp.	dried dill weed
2 tsp.	dried basil
1½ tsp.	salt
1 tsp.	garlic powder
1 tsp.	dried rosemary, crushed
1	egg, slightly beaten

In a small saucepan, heat milk and butter until butter is just melted. Do not allow to get too hot; set aside to cool a bit. In a small bowl, dissolve yeast and sugar in warm water. In a large bowl, combine bread flour and seasonings. Add milk to dry ingredients and mix; add egg and yeast, and mix until smooth. Stir in enough white wheat flour to form a soft dough.

Turn dough onto floured surface; knead until smooth and elastic, about 5 minutes. Place in a large oiled bowl, cover, and allow it to rise in a warm place for 30 minutes.

Divide dough into thirds. Shape each into a 15-inch rope. Place ropes on a greased baking sheet and braid; pinch ends to seal and tuck under. Cover and let rise in a warm place until doubled in size, 30–60 minutes. Preheat oven to 375°F. Bake for 18–20 minutes or until golden brown. Brush with melted butter, if desired. Yields 1 loaf (14–16 slices).

Herb Focaccia Bread

This is my all-time favorite thing to eat with Tomato Basil Bisque with Tortellini (page 105).

1 Tbsp.	yeast
1 tsp.	sugar
1¼ cups	warm water
6 Tbsp.	olive oil, divided
1½ tsp.	salt
½ tsp. each	dried rosemary, oregano, and basil (or 1 tsp. each of fresh)
3 cups	bread flour
¼ cup	Parmesan cheese, shredded or shaved
1 Tbsp.	fresh rosemary (or 1½ tsp. dried)
	coarse sea salt and fresh cracked pepper
1 sm.	tomato, thinly sliced (optional)

Dissolve yeast and sugar in warm water. Add 2 tablespoons oil, salt, dried herbs, and flour. Mix thoroughly. Knead for 5 minutes in your mixing bowl, then let it set for 1 minute. Press dough out into a jelly roll pan and allow it to rise for 20–30 minutes. Preheat oven to 375°F. With the handle of a wooden spoon, make indentions in the top of dough. Brush with 2 tablespoons oil and sprinkle with shaved Parmesan, fresh rosemary, salt, pepper, and tomato, if using. Bake for 20–23 minutes until golden brown. Once the focaccia is out of the oven, drizzle with remaining 2 tablespoons oil. Cut and eat warm—all of it, right on the spot, if you like!

Honey Oatmeal Bread

This has got to be one of the simplest ways to make bread—ever!

For a bread machine:

1 cup	warm water
¼ cup	honey
1⅓ cups	bread flour
¾ cup	whole wheat flour (or 1 cup all-purpose flour)
1 cup	rolled oats
1½ Tbsp.	dry milk
1¼ tsp.	salt
1½ Tbsp.	salted butter, softened
2 Tbsp.	flax seed (optional)
2 tsp.	yeast

Place ingredients in order from top to bottom in bread machine, creating a well for the yeast. Do not let the yeast touch moisture. Set the machine to your normal setting. Yields 1½ lb. loaf.

For a conventional oven:

2 tsp.	yeast
1 cup	warm water
¼ cup	honey
1½ Tbsp.	salted butter, softened
1⅓ cups	bread flour
¾ cup	white wheat flour (or 1 cup all-purpose flour)
1 cup	rolled oats
1½ Tbsp.	dry milk
1¼ tsp.	salt
2 Tbsp.	flax seed (optional)

Dissolve yeast in warm water. Place honey, butter, both flours, oats, dry milk, salt, and flax seed, if using, in a mixing bowl; stir. Add yeast mixture and mix well. Knead in mixer with dough hook for 5 minutes, or knead by hand. Place dough (which will be very sticky) in a well-oiled pan. Allow to rise until double in size, about 35–45 minutes. Punch down, shape into a loaf and place in greased bread pan. Poke the bread dough with a fork about 8–10 times. Cover bread dough and allow to rise until double in size again, approximately 20–30 minutes. Preheat oven to 375°F. Bake for 15 minutes; reduce heat to 350° and bake an additional 10 minutes. Remove from oven and allow bread to set for 10 minutes. Then remove from pan and spread butter on top of your finished loaf of bread, if desired. Yields 1 lb. loaf.

🥐 **And Another Thing . . . And Another Thing . . .** You may use quick oats; however, I prefer rolled oats because they have more nutritional value.

No-Knead Wheat Oatmeal Bread

Bread doesn't get any simpler than this. This loaf has a dense texture and is a little more spongy than bread that is kneaded. It's a perfect last-minute accompaniment to a pot of soup or if you're having impromptu company. It takes ten minutes to mix up, period. I am all about something that is quick but healthy, because I can get too overwhelmed late in my day to think about making bread to go with our dinner meal. This is what you could call wholesome, nutritious, and delicious. It is also the first recipe that helped me view bread baking as a possible task to tackle. It was a small step, and I am so glad I started with this! If the art of baking bread feels like a mountain to you, start with this recipe. I hope it will inspire you to try other yeast breads!

2 tsp.	honey
2⅔ cups	lukewarm water, divided
4 tsp.	yeast
3 Tbsp.	molasses
1½ tsp.	salt
2 Tbsp.	flax seed
2 Tbsp.	wheat bran or germ
1 cup	rolled oats
4 cups	wheat flour

Stir honey into ⅔ cup lukewarm water. Sprinkle yeast over the mixture and set aside for 10 minutes. Combine molasses with ⅔ cup warm water, then combine with yeast mixture. Add salt, flax seed, wheat bran, oats, wheat flour, and remaining 1⅓ cups warm water; stir well. Dough will be sticky. Spread dough evenly into a greased loaf pan. Sprinkle a few oats over top of loaf, if desired. Allow to rise to at least 1 inch above rim of pan, approximately 30 minutes. Bake at 400°F for 10 minutes. Reduce heat to 350°F and bake for an additional 10–15 minutes until golden brown. Allow to cool 10 minutes before turning out of pan. Cool before slicing. Yields 1 nice 1½ lb. loaf or 2 smaller loaves.

🐦 **And Another Thing . . . And Another Thing . . .** When working with yeast, it is very important that the yeast is still active, meaning it is not past its expiration date. Be sure to check your labels. Also be sure to dissolve all the yeast into the water before adding dry ingredients.

Oatmeal Wheat Dinner Rolls

2 cups	water
1 cup	rolled oats
⅓ cup	brown sugar, lightly packed
¼ cup	salted butter
1½ tsp.	salt
2 Tbsp.	yeast
1 tsp.	sugar
½ cup	warm water
1 cup	white wheat flour
3½ cups	bread flour
1	egg, beaten

In a medium saucepan, bring water to a boil. Stir in oats. Reduce heat and simmer uncovered for 1 minute. Stir in brown sugar, butter, and salt. Cool to lukewarm (I like to set it in the refrigerator to chill quickly). In a small bowl, dissolve yeast and sugar in warm water.

In a large mixing bowl, combine 2½ cups of flour and oatmeal mixture; add yeast mixture. Add egg. Beat well. Add remaining flour to form soft dough. The dough will be a little sticky. (It can be a little difficult to work with sticky dough, but sticky dough yields moist rolls!) Knead in mixer with dough hook for 5 minutes. If you don't have a mixer that can do this, turn the dough onto a floured surface and knead until smooth and elastic. Place into a lightly oiled bowl, turning once to oil all sides of the dough. Cover and let rise in a warm place until doubled, about 1 hour. Shape into 24 rolls. Place in 2 greased 9 x 13 baking pans. Cover and let rise until doubled, about 45 minutes. Preheat oven to 350°F. Sprinkle with additional oats, if desired. Bake for 15–20 minutes or until golden. Turn out rolls onto wire racks to cool. Brush melted butter on top of rolls, if desired.

Homemade White Bread with Wheat Flakes

My sister-in-law Heather waltzed into our world in 2003 and wowed us all with her amazing bread making abilities. We are still in awe of them. She always gets asked to bring bread to our family and extended family gatherings. Heather told me that she can remember learning to make this bread when she was a little girl. She said, "I would stand on a chair beside Mama, and she would let me stir until it got too hard for me to stir anymore." These are the stories that fill our lives, stories of daily living that make life rich. When I hear a story like that, I want to talk about life to my children and to their children, and create traditions that build an "altar of remembrance" in their lives. Oh, that God would help us to take those opportunities, do it well, and not burn out in the daily drudgeries of living!

1½ cups	lukewarm water
3 Tbsp.	yeast
½ cup + 1 Tbsp.	raw or white sugar, divided
4 cups	hot water
1 Tbsp.	salt
½ cup	canola oil
1½ cups	wheat flakes, rolled oats, or 7 grain flakes
10–11 cups	bread flour

Mix lukewarm water, yeast, and 1 tablespoon sugar in a small mixing bowl. Stir and set aside until mixture is bubbly. Mix hot water, remaining ½ cup sugar, salt, oil, wheat flakes, and 4 cups bread flour in a large bowl until well blended. Add yeast mixture and mix well. Add remaining flour—just enough that the dough is not too sticky. Roll dough onto countertop and knead for 4–5 minutes or until dough is smooth and a nice consistency. Place in a well-oiled bowl, cover, and let rise in a warm place for 45–60 minutes or until dough is double in size. Punch dough down and divide into 5 equal portions. Shape into loaves. (If you don't have enough bread pans, you can also form these into dinner rolls or hamburger rolls.) Poke the top of each loaf 8–10 times with a fork to release any air pockets that may be in the dough. Cover and let rise again in a warm place for 30 minutes or until double in size. It's important not to allow the bread to rise too much longer than necessary. Otherwise when you slice your bread it will be very crumbly or have large air pockets, and not stay together well. Bake at 375°F for

15 minutes, then reduce heat to 350°F and bake for another 10–15 minutes. Remove loaves from pans and allow to cool on wire rack. Yields 5 small loaves.

🐾 **And Another Thing . . . And Another Thing . . .** I have had to use as much as 14 cups of flour when I make this. It all depends on the weather, how exact you were with your measurements, and the kind of flour you use. If you can handle the bread with well-buttered hands and not have half of the dough left in your fingers, you know you have the right amount of flour. As soon as this bread is baked, I love to cut a big end piece off the warm loaf and place a nice, creamy, yellow pat of butter on top. Beware: you will be addicted for life!

Honey Cinnamon Butter

1 lb.	salted butter, softened
½ cup	honey
1 tsp.	cinnamon

Mix butter, honey, and cinnamon until thoroughly combined. Place into a container and enjoy! It will keep for 4 months in the refrigerator. It is so yummy served on warm biscuits or bread.

Amish Peanut Butter

This is a spread for bread and anything else you want to put it on! My aunt Ruth has made a similar version of this for each of her nieces and nephews at Christmastime. It is so good on anything that calls for peanut butter, including ice cream and pancakes—but it is best of all on homemade bread.

Bring the following ingredients to a rolling boil and then immediately remove from heat:

1¼ cups	brown sugar
2 Tbsp.	pure maple syrup or corn syrup
½ cup	hot water

Cool completely. Add to the cooked mixture and stir thoroughly:

1 cup	marshmallow cream
1½ cups	peanut butter
½ tsp.	maple flavoring, optional

Store in an airtight container. It will keep for 3 months in the refrigerator—if it lasts that long. Yields 3 cups.

> 🐦 **And Another Thing . . . And Another Thing . . .** When it comes to chips, I can eat just one. But when it comes to this divine stuff, I cannot keep my spoon out of the jar. It is so worth the effort to make! However, be advised that excess will cause significant weight gain. We had a customer at The Farmer's Wife who came in and bought significant amounts because she was on a doctor-ordered weight gain regimen. This certainly helped her get to the weight she wanted. I think she was eating a pint every couple of days. It is that good.

Angel Biscuits

These biscuits are buttery and have a quality that makes you grin! And because you can refrigerate these overnight, it is very easy to have a wonderful, light biscuit to serve for breakfast. Want to know what to do with leftover buttermilk from this recipe? Make homemade Buttermilk Ranch Dressing (page 86).

1 Tbsp.	yeast
¼ cup	warm water
½ cup	salted butter, softened
3 Tbsp.	raw or white sugar
1 cup	buttermilk
½ tsp.	baking soda
2¾ cups	flour
1 tsp.	salt
1½ tsp.	baking powder

Preheat oven to 400°F. Dissolve yeast in warm water. Cream butter and sugar, add buttermilk, baking soda, and dissolved yeast mixture. Stir in flour, salt, and baking powder. Roll out to at least 1-inch thick and cut into desired size. No rising is required. Bake for 12–15 minutes on greased baking sheet. You may add butter to the tops of the biscuits when they come out of the oven. Yields 18–20 biscuits.

And Another Thing . . . And Another Thing . . . This recipe is a perfect night-before kind of recipe. Mix recipe up and place cut biscuits onto greased pans. Cover with plastic wrap that has been sprayed with cooking spray and place in the refrigerator. Pull out the biscuits and allow them to sit at room temperature for 30 minutes before following above baking instructions. You may need to add 5–7 minutes to the baking time if the pan is cold when you place it in the oven.

So here is my honest confession: before this cookbook I stayed away from all recipes with yeast. I owned a bakery so you would naturally think I bake bread: wrong! I just had amazing bakers that made me look good! This cookbook project has forced me to embrace yeast recipes. I still feel bad about an order of biscuits that I sent out of The Farmer's Wife back in the early days. If I would have had this recipe, I would have sent them out with confidence, knowing the customer would not be disappointed. While I learned a life lesson from that experience, it still humbles me every time I think of it. I wish I could make it right.

Food for Thought

The day I reworked the Angel Biscuit recipe, I was beyond tired. I had been in the kitchen all week rolling out recipe after recipe and washing dish after dish. I was also five weeks pregnant and quite sick because of it, and had hosted a baby shower in our home for forty people that week. Our son Camden had woken from his afternoon nap that day with a fresh wave of energy and fresh vision to help me roll out these biscuits. When those words, "Mom, I want to help you," came out of his little mouth, I almost gave him all the reasons why today would not be a good day even as he busily pushed his stool over to assist me. He picked up his red play-dough cookie cutter that I had been using and looked at it oddly. I stopped myself and said, "Of course you can help me, son." And so we went to work, he with his little spatula and flour mess, and I with a heart full from the happy smiles I received from him—simply because I'd said yes.

Will he be a chef someday, milk cows, run a business, be a doctor, or be a pastor? His options are endless. Whenever that day arrives, I know little moments like these will be foundational to who he becomes. He is being shaped today in little places of his heart simply because of these "angel biscuit" opportunities. That day, I found such delight in being a mom to this flour-faced little boy who has won my heart a thousand times over. These are the moments I have to pour Jesus into his life. As a mom, you know what I am talking about. You know them when you have them. We had the best time together making Angel Biscuits. God was speaking to me in that moment, and I am so grateful I listened and didn't let my fatigue get in the way. I am excited about all the future "angel biscuit" moments. The key is to keep my heart open to look for them. What are ways you could share moments today with someone who needs you?

3

Spring Salads and Dressings

When setting a table, the sweetest, simple touches can make a difference. A folded linen napkin needs only a tiny spring flower laid on top to make it extra special. Or place a fresh bouquet of daffodils in a Mason jar to adorn your table. All of these "fresh" reminders of life awaken us. In the spring, our senses are completely aware of the fresh waking of earth when we walk outside and breathe deeply. We can feel the world coming alive, like something is ready to break loose. Often our hearts go through seasons, and we need spring to come and blow its fresh wind into our hearts. In the spring we find fresh energy to put one foot in front of the other.

A simple strategy that allows me to have fresh lettuce all spring is to do multiple plantings of several varieties of lettuce, spaced two weeks apart. Then I have a wide variety of greens constantly growing to cut for a fresh salad. Walking out my back door to my tiny little garden plot of fresh greens is so invigorating! If you don't have a garden plot, try planting lettuce in a pot. You will be so happy you did!

Apple Pecan Salad with Sweet and Sour Dressing

1 bunch	romaine lettuce, washed and chopped
1	Gala apple, sliced thin (do not peel)
½ cup	pecan halves
	red onion ringlets (to taste)
½ cup	feta cheese (or blue cheese)
¼ cup	Sweet and Sour Dressing (see recipe page 87)

Toss all ingredients together in a serving bowl, and you're ready to enjoy.

Caribbean Chicken Salad

My sister-in-law Naomi introduced me to a version of this tasty and attractive salad. We love to serve this to our guests, especially in the spring and summer.

4	boneless, skinless chicken breasts
16 oz.	honey Dijon salad dressing
1 head	red leaf lettuce, cleaned and chopped
1 cup	canned black beans, drained and rinsed
¼ cup	red onion, diced
½ cup	cashew halves, unsalted
1 (11 oz.) can	mandarin oranges, drained
1	mango, peeled and diced
½ cup	cheddar cheese, shredded
½ cup	Monterey Jack cheese, shredded

Place chicken breasts in a lidded container or resealable plastic bag; pour half of the honey Dijon salad dressing over the chicken, turning to coat. Marinate for 1–2 hours (optional). Grill chicken right before ready to place on salad.

Place chopped lettuce on dinner plates. Layer with black beans, red onions, cashews, mandarin oranges, and mango. Slice cooked chicken breasts into strips and place 1 breast on top of each salad. Top each salad with a sprinkle of both cheeses. Serve with remaining honey Dijon salad dressing or other salad dressing of your choice. Serves 4.

🕊 **And Another Thing . . . And Another Thing . . .** This salad is a great, filling entrée. Serve with breadsticks or a bread you really enjoy and you will have people raving about their dinner experience.

Cashew and Swiss Salad

10 cups	lettuce (red leaf, green leaf, or romaine), chopped
1 cup	cashew halves
4 oz.	Swiss cheese, julienned
4	green onions, diced
2 cups	broccoli, chopped
1 cup	strawberries, sliced (or ½ cup dried cranberries)
1	red pear, sliced thin (do not peel)

Dressing:

⅓ cup	white vinegar
½ cup	raw or white sugar
2 tsp.	mustard
1 tsp.	onion, grated
¾ cup	olive oil
dash	salt
1 tsp.	poppy seeds

Toss together the lettuce, cashews, Swiss cheese, green onions, broccoli, strawberries, and pear. For the dressing, blend vinegar, sugar, mustard, onion, oil, and salt in blender until sugar is dissolved. Gradually add poppy seeds. Pour half of dressing over salad and toss. You will have enough dressing left to use for another salad. It will keep for 8–10 weeks in the refrigerator. Serves 8–10.

🕊 **And Another Thing . . . And Another Thing . . .** Add grilled chicken to this salad to serve it as an entrée.

Cranberry Salad

We eat this from November to January. I buy cranberries as long as the season allows. I usually keep a gelatin like this in our refrigerator to go with evening meals. This is a wonderful way to top off our dinner without too many extra calories. It is simple, festive, and will keep for 1 week in the refrigerator.

1 (6 oz.) pkg.	raspberry gelatin
⅓ cup	raw or white sugar
1 cup	boiling water
2 cups	fresh whole cranberries, crushed and blended with ⅓ cup water
1 (11 oz.) can	mandarin oranges, undrained
1 cup	apple, peeled and diced
1 (8 oz.) can	crushed pineapple, undrained

Dissolve gelatin and sugar in boiling water. Once gelatin mixture is completely dissolved, add cranberries, mandarin oranges, apple, and pineapple. Pour into gelatin mold or a dish of choice and refrigerate until set. Serves 10–12.

Grape Salad

2 cups	whipping cream
1 cup	powdered sugar
4 oz.	cream cheese, softened
1 cup	vanilla yogurt
2 Tbsp.	orange or lemon juice
14 cups	red and green grapes, well drained

In a bowl, beat whipping cream until soft peaks form and add powdered sugar. In another bowl beat cream cheese until soft, and add yogurt and orange juice. Fold in whipped cream. Stir in grapes. Serves 12–14.

Layered Broccoli Cranberry Salad

This salad is so pretty layered in a clear bowl due to the contrasting colors. I really like it because the dressing base is plain yogurt, which is healthier and lower in fat than sour cream.

6 cups	fresh broccoli florets (or broccoli and cauliflower)
⅓ cup	red onion, diced
1 cup	bacon, cooked and diced
1½ cups	cheddar cheese, shredded
⅔ cup	dried cranberries
½ cup	sliced almonds or chopped walnuts

Dressing:

¾ cup	plain yogurt
¼ cup	honey
¾ cup	mayonnaise
1 Tbsp.	balsamic vinegar
½ tsp.	cracked black pepper

Layer half the broccoli and red onion in a clear bowl. In a small bowl, whisk together yogurt, honey, mayonnaise, vinegar, and black pepper and spread half of the dressing evenly over the broccoli and red onion. Then add half of the bacon, cheese, cranberries, and nuts. Repeat layers. Serves 6–8.

And Another Thing . . . And Another Thing . . . To get 1 cup of cooked, diced bacon, you'll probably use about ¾ lb., depending on the thickness of your bacon. If you do not like to use bacon you can substitute an equal amount of pecans and omit the other nuts.

Pecan–Ramen Noodle Salad

1 (3 oz.) pkg.	chicken flavored ramen noodles
2 Tbsp.	salted butter
1 cup	pecan halves
6 cups	romaine lettuce, chopped
3 cups	broccoli, chopped
1	red bell pepper, cut into rings

Dressing:

½ cup	raw or white sugar
¼ cup	vinegar
½ cup	olive oil
½ tsp.	pepper
1 tsp.	salt

Crush ramen noodles. Set seasoning packet aside. In a large skillet, brown crushed ramen noodles and pecans in butter for 7–10 minutes; set aside to cool. For the dressing, in a small saucepan heat sugar and vinegar until sugar is dissolved. Cool a bit and add remaining dressing ingredients, including the ramen seasoning packet.

Mix lettuce and broccoli together and place in bowl; toss with half of the dressing. Lay red pepper rings on top and sprinkle with half of the pecan mixture. Serve immediately. You will have enough dressing and pecan mixture for another salad. Serves 5–6.

Spinach Salad with Mandarin Oranges

10 cups	spinach or salad greens
1 lb.	bacon, cooked and crumbled
	red onion, sliced (to taste)
½ cup	almonds, sliced
3	hard boiled eggs, diced
1 (11 oz.) can	mandarin oranges, drained

Dressing:

⅓ cup	raw or white sugar
2½ Tbsp.	vinegar
2½ Tbsp.	honey
½ tsp.	paprika
½ tsp.	salt
½ tsp.	ground mustard
½ tsp.	celery seed
1 tsp.	garlic powder
1 Tbsp.	lemon juice
¼ cup	olive oil

Stir all salad ingredients together. For dressing, combine the first 9 ingredients in a saucepan over medium-high heat and cook, stirring, until sugar is dissolved. Remove from heat and add oil. Mix well. You can serve this dressing hot or cold. Right before serving salad, add dressing and toss. Serves 8–10.

🐌 **And Another Thing . . . And Another Thing . . .** If you cook bacon in the oven at 400° for 15–20 minutes on a tinfoil-lined baking pan, cleanup is very easy.

Summer Bounty Salad

To me there is something so fun about a dish that looks bright and is healthy! This has to be one of my favorite sides to eat with grilled chicken. If you want to have Sunday guests but don't want to spend a lot of time in the kitchen to make it happen, this is the perfect dish!

⅓ cup	olive oil
¼ cup	balsamic vinegar
1 Tbsp.	chili powder
½ tsp.	salt
½ tsp.	fresh cracked pepper
2 Tbsp.	fresh basil, minced
1 cup	cucumber, diced (I like to peel my cucumbers)
1	green bell pepper, diced
½ cup	red onion, minced
2 cups	tomatoes, diced
1 (15.5 oz.) can	black beans, drained and rinsed
1 (16 oz.) can	corn
1 cup	feta cheese

Mix together olive oil, vinegar, chili powder, salt, and pepper; set aside. Place basil, cucumber, green pepper, onion, tomatoes, black beans, corn, and feta cheese in a bowl. Pour dressing over top. Serves 6–8.

🌿 **And Another Thing . . . And Another Thing . . .** If you have leftover corn from corn on the cob, cut it off; freeze it and save it for this recipe.

Spinach, Ranch, and Bacon Salad

This is a five-ingredient salad that is simple and so delicious to take to a carry-in or picnic.

1 (12 oz.) pkg.	cheese tortellini
8 cups	fresh spinach (or 2 6-oz. pkgs.)
8–10 slices	bacon, cooked and chopped
1 pt.	grape tomatoes, washed and halved
1½ cups	ranch salad dressing

Cook tortellini per package directions. Drain and cool. Toss all ingredients together except salad dressing. Wait to add salad dressing until right before serving. Serves 8–10.

🐦 **And Another Thing . . . And Another Thing . . .** Need a fun dish to serve at a summertime picnic? Take pint Mason jars and place this salad into each one. Each guest will have their own personal serving of salad. It's a fun, inexpensive way to use what you have on hand to add an extra touch to a summer party.

83

Fiesta Corn Bread Salad

This is a one-dish meal. It's perfect for dinner and is very substantial. It's a wonderful dish to make for carry-ins.

1 (8.5 oz.) pkg.	corn bread mix
1 (4 oz.) can	chopped green chiles
½ tsp.	dried oregano
½ tsp.	cumin
1 cup	mayonnaise
1½ cups	plain yogurt
1 (1 oz.) pkg.	dry ranch dressing mix
2 Tbsp.	fresh cilantro, chopped
8–10 cups	lettuce, torn
2 (15 oz.) cans	black beans, drained and rinsed
1 cup	whole kernel corn, drained
2 cups	cheddar cheese, shredded
½ cup	red onion, chopped
1 cup	green bell pepper, chopped
2 lg.	tomatoes, chopped and drained
½ lb.	bacon, cooked and crumbled
1 (3.8 oz.) can	black olives

Preheat oven to 400°F. Mix cornbread mix according to package directions, then add chiles, oregano, and cumin. Bake according to package directions. Set aside to cool. Mix together mayonnaise, yogurt, dressing mix, and cilantro; set aside. Cut corn bread into 1-inch squares. In a large (20 qt.) glass serving bowl, place half of the lettuce, then add half of the corn bread and half of the beans, dressing mixture, corn, cheese, onion, green pepper, tomatoes, bacon, and olives. Repeat layers. Cover and refrigerate for 2 hours. Garnish with spring onions or fresh chives, if desired. Serves 12–15.

🍝 **And Another Thing . . . And Another Thing . . .** You can substitute the Buttermilk Ranch Dressing on page 86 for the mayonnaise, plain yogurt, and ranch dressing mix in this recipe.

My new favorite trick is to always have lettuce ready to use when I need it. I struggle to get fresh salads on the table if I first have to wash and cut the lettuce—and it's time for dinner to be served. I have great intentions earlier in my day, but at dinnertime it is just easier to grab a bag of frozen vegetables and let my stovetop do the work. However, I have found that this has saved the day and the lettuce from ending in the compost bin: when I use a head of lettuce for the first time I wash and cut it all. The key is to store it in lidded glass quart jars in your refrigerator. Voila! When you want to make that salad you will already have ready-to-use lettuce for a fraction of the price of precut lettuce. If you drain it well before you cut it, the lettuce will keep for a week or more in lidded glass jars.

Blue Cheese Dressing or Dip

1 cup	mayonnaise
3 Tbsp.	milk (more if you prefer a thinner dressing)
1 Tbsp.	fresh lemon juice
1 tsp.	dried minced onion
2 tsp.	sugar
½ tsp.	Worcestershire sauce
¼ tsp.	dry ground mustard
½ tsp.	salt
¼ tsp.	fresh ground black pepper
¾ cup	blue cheese, crumbled

Mix ingredients together in order given. Refrigerate for 2–4 hours. Yields 1½ cups.

🕊 **And Another Thing . . . And Another Thing . . .** Replace the blue cheese with feta cheese, and when summer tomatoes are in over-abundance, slice a few on a dinner plate and drizzle with this dressing.

Buttermilk Ranch Dressing

The benefit of making your own dressing is that your ingredients are fresh, without added preservatives or MSG. These kinds of simple, healthy choices are what I love to serve my family.

1 cup	plain yogurt
½ cup	buttermilk
½ cup	mayonnaise
1 tsp.	garlic salt
1 tsp.	dried basil (or 2 tsp. fresh)
2 tsp.	parsley flakes (or 3 tsp. fresh)
½ tsp.	dill weed
¼ tsp.	fresh cracked pepper
¼ tsp.	paprika
1 Tbsp.	dried minced onion (or 2 tsp. fresh)

Combine all ingredients with a whisk and mix until smooth. If you would like a thicker dressing to use as a dip, add ½ cup more mayonnaise. Yields 2½ cups.

Orange Poppy Seed Dressing

This is excellent served over a spinach salad with bacon, pecans, and red peppers. Sometimes you just need a different twist to a salad. This is it!

¼ cup	honey
¼ cup	apple cider vinegar
¼ tsp.	salt
⅛ tsp.	fresh cracked pepper
1 tsp.	orange zest
⅓ cup	orange juice concentrate
2 tsp.	poppy seeds
¾ cup	olive oil

Whisk honey, vinegar, salt, pepper, orange zest, and orange juice concentrate until well blended, or shake in a lidded glass jar until mixed. Add poppy seeds and oil and shake or whisk until well mixed. Pour over salad when ready to serve. Store leftovers in the refrigerator. Dressing will keep for 4–6 months. Yields 1½ cups.

Sweet and Sour Dressing

1 cup	olive oil
¼ cup	vinegar
¼ cup	water
1 cup	raw or white sugar
½ cup	onion, minced fine
¼ cup	mayonnaise
1 Tbsp.	prepared mustard
1 tsp.	salt
½ tsp.	black pepper
1 tsp.	celery seed

Blend olive oil, vinegar, water, sugar, and onion in a blender or food processor. Then add remaining ingredients and pulse just until mixed well. Will store in refrigerator for 6–8 weeks. Yields 3¼ cups.

Food for Thought

I have been thinking a lot about grace these days, asking myself: What does it look like to be a woman of grace? What does it look like in my life to offer the women around me grace? I believe it includes things like overlooking easy opportunities to take offense. And it includes offering my friend grace when I hear about something she did that doesn't make sense to me. I have been caught—caught in the snarls of my own mind, and my limited perspective. Silly little things people say and do can trip me up. Maybe a casual friend *was* short with me, but I don't know what's going on in her world. For me to take those little things and let them be the bedrock of how I feel about our friendship will only wear me out. I have discovered that when I offer my friends grace, I am aware of the overwhelming grace of God afresh in my life. I want to live here, to stay in this place of giving and receiving grace. It's such a delightful place for my heart to be.

4

Summer Sandwiches and Winter Soups

JOY is the realest reality, the fullest life, and JOY is always given, never grasped. God gives gifts and I give thanks and I unwrap the gift given: JOY.

Ann Voskamp

Summer and fall were delightful days growing up on the farm. Sure, we worked when we didn't want to, and would rather have ridden our bikes—and for sure our dad, a bi-vocational pastor, was busier than any family man should have been and didn't have enough time for us. We floundered through our issues. And there were many days I didn't feel like picking the green beans or cleaning the house, but as I moved on to my own adult world, I realized how wonderfully delicious those days truly were. Days filled with root beer floats, fresh peaches and blueberries, and nights around the campfire in the backyard with more roasted marshmallows than the dentist would approve. Summers included weekend camping trips with our church group and a precious family trip to Canada to a hand-hewn cabin. I will treasure memories of fall nights raking leaves, and hot summer afternoons on the ball field Dad allowed us to make in the hay field. These are small but important things that make my life rich and remind me I am loved deeply. As I continue to unwrap the gifts given from memories of my past, I am experiencing joy!

Garden Herb Grilled Burgers

These burgers are so fun to make if you have fresh herbs growing in your garden. Sometimes you may wonder if it is worth it to grow all the herbs you do if you are not using them all the time, but when you can go out to your garden and cut off the fresh ingredients required for this recipe it is so worth it.

1 lb.	ground beef
2 Tbsp.	fresh parsley (or 1 Tbsp. dried)
1 Tbsp.	fresh chives (or 1½ tsp. dried)
1 Tbsp.	fresh basil (or 1½ tsp. dried)
1	garlic clove, minced
1 tsp.	Worcestershire sauce
½ tsp.	salt
½ tsp.	fresh cracked pepper
1	egg
½ cup	bread crumbs (or oatmeal)
4	hamburger buns

Mix together all ingredients except buns and form into 4 patties. Grill over medium heat for 5–7 minutes each side or until preferred doneness. Assemble with buns and garnish with lettuce, tomatoes, red onion, and mayonnaise as desired. Serves 4.

Farmer's BLT

BLTs and root beer floats made with ice cream from the local ice cream shop found their way into our farmhouse kitchen many times. It still blows me away how those foods take me right back to my childhood summers. It may not be what the USDA food pyramid would approve as a well-balanced nutritional dinner, but it was still probably more nutritional than eating fast food. Cheese is what makes these sandwiches extra yummy.

1 lb.	bacon
¼ cup	mayonnaise
8 pieces	bread, toasted (homemade bread is the best)
4 slices	Swiss or provolone cheese
	garden fresh tomatoes
	fresh lettuce

Cook bacon until crispy; extra crispy is best. Toast bread and spread mayonnaise on each piece. Layer bacon, cheese, tomatoes, and lettuce. Cut each sandwich diagonally and enjoy! Serves 4.

Grilled Caesar Burgers

1 lb.	ground beef
1 Tbsp.	fresh parsley, minced (or 1½ tsp. dried)
½ cup	Caesar dressing, divided
½ tsp.	salt
1 sm.	Vidalia onion, thinly sliced
	romaine lettuce leaves
	tomato slices
	fresh shaved Parmesan cheese
4	sandwich buns, grilled

Mix together ground beef, parsley, half of Caesar dressing, and salt. Form into 4 patties; set aside. Place onion on a piece of tinfoil. Drizzle remaining Caesar dressing over onion. Fold foil up and over onion to form a pocket, sealing the edges so it doesn't leak. Place burgers and onion pack on grill. Grill burgers approximately 5–7 minutes per side or until desired doneness. Grill onions until softened, about 8–10 minutes. Garnish burgers with onion, lettuce, tomatoes, and Parmesan. These burgers are very moist.

Turkey Club Sandwich with Cranberry Mayonnaise

4	onion rolls (or bread of your choice)
½ lb.	turkey breast
4 slices	Swiss cheese
8 slices	bacon, cooked
½	Gala apple, sliced thin
4 pieces	lettuce

Cranberry mayonnaise:

½ cup	mayonnaise
½ cup	cranberry sauce (any kind)
1 Tbsp.	Dijon mustard
2 Tbsp.	pecans, chopped
1 Tbsp.	honey

For cranberry mayonnaise, mix all ingredients together until well blended. Spread 1 tablespoon cranberry mayonnaise on each half of roll. Layer each sandwich roll with turkey, cheese, bacon, apple, and lettuce. Serve and enjoy. Refrigerate leftover cranberry mayonnaise; it will keep for 1–2 months in the refrigerator. Serves 4.

Ham and Cheese Sticky Buns

This dish is wonderful to serve at a birthday party or as an appetizer!

¾ lb.	deli ham (I prefer Virginia baked ham), sliced thin
½ lb.	provolone or farmer's cheese, sliced thin
1 dz.	mini sandwich rolls

Sauce ingredients:

½ cup	salted butter
2 Tbsp.	poppy seeds
¼ cup	brown sugar
2 Tbsp.	Worcestershire sauce
2 Tbsp.	prepared yellow mustard
1 Tbsp.	onion flakes

Preheat oven to 350°F. Place bottom halves of the sandwich rolls in a baking dish. Layer ham and then cheese on top. In a medium saucepan, mix all sauce ingredients together and boil for 2 minutes. Pour sauce mixture evenly over top of the rolls, then add the top half of each sandwich roll to form complete sandwiches. Cover dish with foil and bake for 15 minutes. Serve immediately. Serves 6.

🐾 **And Another Thing . . . And Another Thing . . .** These can easily be an entrée. They pair well with soup and salad and are so yummy!

Thai Turkey Roll Ups

Peanut butter mayonnaise:

¼ cup	peanut butter
¼ cup	mayonnaise
2 Tbsp.	brown sugar
2	garlic cloves, crushed
2 tsp.	soy sauce
2 tsp.	lime juice
1 tsp.	ground ginger
pinch	red pepper

Wraps:

4 (10 in.)	flour tortillas
8–12 slices	turkey breast
¼ cup	fresh cilantro, chopped
1 cup	red cabbage, shredded
½ cup	carrots, shredded
1 cup	red bell pepper, julienned

Prepare peanut butter mayonnaise by mixing all ingredients together until well blended. Spread mayonnaise evenly onto each tortilla. Divide turkey, cilantro, cabbage, carrots, and bell peppers equally among the four tortillas. Roll up each wrap. Place in plastic wrap if you're not eating it right away. If serving immediately, place a toothpick in each of them to keep the wraps together. Yields 4 wraps.

🐦 **And Another Thing . . . And Another Thing . . .** A key to rolling wraps is to roll them up in the same direction you placed the turkey the long way on the wrap. I also like to use colored toothpicks to keep them rolled up for the duration of serving time. Once you have cut the wraps to your liking, either in halves or in thirds, place a toothpick all the way through each section of wrap to hold it together.

Black Bean Soup

This recipe would never have grabbed my attention if it weren't for Panera Bread's black bean soup. They make a great black bean soup, and here is a somewhat similar version.

3 (15.5 oz.) cans	black beans, rinsed and drained
4 cups	chicken broth, divided
1 cup	onion, minced
3	garlic cloves, minced
½ cup	celery, diced
½ cup	carrots, shredded
2 tsp.	chili powder
1 tsp.	cumin
1 tsp.	dried oregano
½ tsp.	black pepper
1 tsp.	salt
	red pepper flakes, to taste

Garnishes:

½ cup	cheddar cheese, shredded
½ cup	tomatoes, chopped
¼ cup	green onions, chopped

Place a third of the black beans in a blender with ½ cup chicken broth. Blend well. Pour into slow cooker. Stir in remaining black beans, and add remaining ingredients. Cook on low for 6 hours.

Serve the soup with garnishes as desired. Crusty bread is always great with this soup! Serves 4.

Chicken, Mushroom, and Wild Rice Soup

We only served soups at The Farmer's Wife in the fall and winter. On the very first day there was an autumn chill in the air, our phones would start ringing with customers wondering when the "soup of the day" would begin. I cannot explain it, but just the smell of onions browning in butter grabbed people's attention and they would walk out having bought more than they came in for. I think onions and butter take us back, igniting our senses to recall memories of our mother's cooking. Good soups develop over time. If you're hosting a party on Friday, prepare the soup on Tuesday and allow the flavors to steep.

¼ cup	olive oil or salted butter
1 cup	onion, diced
1–1½ cups	celery, diced
1–1½ cups	carrots, diced
1½ cups	fresh mushrooms, sliced
4	garlic cloves, minced
¼ cup	salted butter
½ cup	all-purpose flour
10 cups	chicken broth
2 cups	cooked and shredded chicken
5–6 cups	long grain and wild rice, cooked
2 Tbsp.	chicken bouillon (optional)
½ tsp.	salt
1 tsp.	fresh cracked pepper
1 cup	half-and-half
3 Tbsp.	fresh parsley (or 1½ Tbsp. dried)

Melt ¼ cup of oil or butter in a large skillet; add onions, celery, and carrots. Cook over medium-high heat until tender, about 8–10 minutes. Add mushrooms and garlic and cook until softened.

In a large stockpot, melt ¼ cup butter over medium-high heat; whisk in flour and stir. Gradually add half of the chicken broth and cook about 6–8 minutes or until mixture is thickened. Be sure to stir often so it doesn't get lumpy. Stir in vegetable mixture, chicken, rice, remaining broth, bouillon, salt, and pepper. Cook, stirring occasionally, 5–10 minutes or until thoroughly heated. Do not boil. Add half-and-half. Garnish with parsley and serve. Serves 12–16.

Simple Sloppy Joes

A slice of cheese on top of an open-faced sloppy Joe sandwich is the ticket to turning something ordinary into something extraordinary. On busy days on the farm this was our supper, and I still enjoy a sandwich like this.

1½ lbs.	hamburger
½ cup	onion, chopped fine
⅓ cup	oatmeal
1 tsp.	salt
½ cup	milk
2 Tbsp.	brown sugar
1 Tbsp.	vinegar
2 Tbsp.	Worcestershire sauce
1 cup	ketchup
6	potato hamburger rolls
6 slices	provolone or American cheese

Put all ingredients except for rolls and cheese in a slow cooker. The meat does not have to be precooked. Cook on high for 3 hours. Stir occasionally. Serve open-faced on rolls and top each with a slice of cheese. Serves 6.

And Another Thing . . . And Another Thing . . . You can also cook this on your stovetop. Allow to simmer for 35–40 minutes on low so that the flavors can blend beautifully.

Cream of Chicken Soup with Vegetables

Let the smell of simmering soup fill your kitchen with the aromas of a cozy season.

1 (16 oz.) pkg.	frozen mixed vegetables
½ cup	water
1 tsp.	salt, divided
¼ cup	salted butter
¼ cup	all-purpose flour
2 cups	half-and-half
2	garlic cloves, minced
2 cups	chicken, cooked and shredded
4 cups	chicken broth
1 Tbsp.	fresh parsley (or 1½ tsp. dried)
1 tsp.	dried basil (or 2 tsp. fresh)
½ tsp.	fresh cracked black pepper

Cook frozen vegetables in water and ½ tsp. salt until tender. Melt butter in saucepan over medium heat; whisk in flour. Gradually add half-and-half, whisking constantly. Add garlic and bring mixture to a boil. Immediately add undrained vegetables, chicken, chicken broth, parsley, basil, pepper, and remaining salt. Heat through. Serve immediately. Serves 4–6.

Santa Fe Chicken Soup

1 cup	onion, chopped
½ cup	sweet red pepper, chopped
½ cup	green bell pepper, chopped
4	garlic cloves, minced
3 Tbsp.	salted butter or olive oil
1 (7 oz.) can	diced green chiles, undrained
8 cups	chicken broth
1 cup	salsa
2 (15 oz.) cans	cannellini (white kidney) beans, drained and rinsed
3 cups	chicken, cooked and shredded
1 tsp.	cumin
2 tsp.	chili powder
1 tsp.	salt
½ tsp.	fresh cracked pepper
½	fresh lime

Garnish:

green onions, diced

cheddar cheese, shredded

tortilla chips

In a large stockpot, cook onion, peppers, and garlic in butter or oil until vegetables are tender. Add chiles and sauté for 2 minutes. Add chicken broth, salsa, beans, and chicken. Bring to a boil; reduce heat to low and simmer for 20 minutes, stirring occasionally. Add cumin, chili powder, salt, and pepper. Right before serving, squeeze juice from lime into hot soup. Serve with garnishes. Serves 6–8.

Fresh Corn and Chicken Chowder

What makes this soup so silky is the potato flakes. Typically soup is thickened with flour or cornstarch, but I like to use potato flakes in this soup. If your chicken is fully cooked, this soup only takes 15 minutes to prep. On busy nights short cooking times are always a plus!

8 cups	chicken broth
1 cup	onion, diced
1 cup	green or red bell pepper, diced
2	garlic cloves, minced
2 cups	chicken, cooked and diced
2 cups	fresh corn kernels (or 1 15-oz. can corn, drained)
1 tsp.	salt (optional)
½ tsp.	cracked pepper
1 Tbsp.	dried chives (or 2 Tbsp. fresh)
2 Tbsp.	fresh parsley
¼ tsp.	red pepper flakes
1 Tbsp.	chicken bouillon (more or less to taste)
2½ cups	mashed potato flakes
2 cups	milk

Place chicken broth, onion, pepper, and garlic in stockpot. Cook until vegetables are softened. Add chicken, corn, spices, and bouillon and heat through. Add potato flakes and milk. Heat just until hot; do not boil. Serve with shredded cheddar cheese and additional red pepper, if desired. Serves 6–8.

🐓 **And Another Thing . . . And Another Thing . . .** You may also use raw chicken breast; just dice and cook in the chicken broth along with the vegetables until fully cooked.

Cheddar Potato Chowder

2½ cups	chicken broth
3 cups	potatoes, diced
½ cup	carrots, shredded
½ cup	celery, diced
¼ cup	onion, diced
2	garlic cloves, minced
½ tsp.	salt
½ tsp.	black pepper
1 Tbsp.	fresh parsley, minced (or 1½ tsp. dried)
1 Tbsp.	fresh chives, minced (or 1½ tsp. dried)
1 cup	bacon, cooked and diced (about ¾ lb.)

Cheese sauce:

¼ cup	salted butter
¼ cup	flour
2½ cups	milk or half-and-half
2 cups	cheddar cheese, shredded

Garnishes:

½ cup	green onions, diced
½ cup	cheddar cheese, shredded
½ cup	croutons

In a large stockpot, combine chicken broth, potatoes, carrots, celery, onion, garlic, salt, and pepper. Boil over medium heat, covered, for 10 minutes.

For cheese sauce, melt butter in a medium saucepan over medium-high heat; add flour and stir, about 1 minute. Slowly add milk. Cook until thickened and bubbly, about 3 minutes, stirring constantly. Add cheese and stir until melted.

Add cheese sauce to soup base. Heat completely. Add parsley, chives, and bacon. Serve with green onions, cheddar cheese, and croutons. Serves 4.

Spinach, Meatball, and Tortellini Soup

This is a rustic version of a fancy dish. I would have never guessed it but I think this has become my favorite soup EVER!

1 lb.	ground beef
1 lb.	ground turkey
1 (10 oz.) pkg.	frozen chopped spinach, thawed and drained
1 tsp.	salt
½ tsp.	pepper
1 tsp.	fresh garlic, minced
2 Tbsp.	dried Italian seasoning
2	eggs
½ cup	bread crumbs
¼ cup	olive oil or salted butter
1 cup	onion, finely chopped
2 cups	carrots, finely chopped
2 cups	celery, finely chopped
10 cups	beef broth
2 (16 oz.) cans	diced tomatoes
2 (16 oz.) cans	kidney beans, drained and rinsed
2 tsp.	dried oregano
2 tsp.	dried basil
1 (9 oz. or more) pkg.	cheese tortellini
	Parmesan cheese, shaved, for garnish

Combine beef, turkey, spinach, salt, pepper, garlic, Italian seasoning, eggs, and bread crumbs. Form into 1-inch balls and place on a baking sheet (I like to line the baking sheet with foil to keep the mess contained). Bake at 350°F for 40 minutes.

Heat oil or butter in a large stockpot and sauté onions, carrots, and celery until softened. Add broth, tomatoes, kidney beans, oregano, and basil. Bring to a boil. Add meatballs and tortellini and simmer for 10 minutes. Serve with Parmesan cheese. Serves 12–15.

Slow cooker version: place cooked meatballs and all remaining ingredients except tortellini in the slow cooker on low heat for 5–6 hours or high for 3 hours. Add tortellini the last 30 minutes. This soup is very thick and filling.

🐦 **And Another Thing . . . And Another Thing . . .** This is a great way to get some hidden nutrition into your family's diet. This soup freezes very well; however, if you freeze it do not add the tortellini until you are ready to reheat and serve. The tortellini tends to disintegrate if left in the broth too long.

Beef and Barley Soup

3	garlic cloves, minced
2 cups	onion, chopped
1 cup	carrot, chopped
1 cup	celery, chopped
3 Tbsp.	salted butter
1 lb.	beef roast, cubed
8 cups	beef broth
½ cup	pearl barley, uncooked
2 cups	mushrooms, sliced (optional)
2 Tbsp.	fresh parsley (or 1 Tbsp. dried)
½ cup	half-and-half

In a large stockpot, sauté garlic, onion, carrot, and celery in butter for 5 minutes. Add beef and sauté for 3 more minutes, then add broth and barley. Bring to a boil, and boil for 5 minutes; reduce heat and add mushrooms. Simmer for at least 2 hours. Right before serving, stir in the parsley and half-and-half. Serves 6–8.

🐦 **And Another Thing . . . And Another Thing . . .** You can also prepare this in a slow cooker. Place all ingredients except parsley and half-and-half in the slow cooker and cook on low for 6–8 hours or high for 4 hours. Right before serving, stir in parsley and half-and-half.

Old-Fashioned Beef Stew

While chicken noodle is queen of all soups, you will not be disappointed by this hearty dish.

1 lb.	boneless beef chuck, cut in 1-inch cubes
2 Tbsp.	flour
½ tsp.	fresh cracked black pepper
2 Tbsp.	olive oil
2 lg.	onions, coarsely chopped
3 lg.	baking potatoes, peeled and cubed
1–2 cups	whole, small mushrooms (optional)
8–10	carrots, peeled and chopped
2 stalks	celery, coarsely chopped
6 whole	garlic cloves
2 cups	beef broth
1	bay leaf
1 Tbsp.	chili powder
1½ tsp.	salt
½ tsp.	dried thyme
⅓ cup	fresh parsley, minced

Place beef, flour, and pepper in a resealable plastic bag; shake to coat well. In a large skillet, heat oil over medium-high heat and brown beef for 4–5 minutes, stirring frequently. Remove from heat.

Add onions, potatoes, mushrooms, carrots, celery, and garlic to a slow cooker. Place meat on top. Add beef broth, bay leaf, chili powder, salt, and thyme. Cook on low for 6–8 hours or high for 3–4 hours. Add parsley for the last 30 minutes of cooking time. Serves 6–8.

🐦 **And Another Thing . . . And Another Thing . . .** If you are in a super hurry to get this dish in the slow cooker, you can eliminate the step of browning the beef.

Tomato Basil Bisque with Tortellini

To me this is comfort food at its best! The tortellini in this soup is just the ticket to perfection. I usually use cheese tortellini, but feel free to try other kinds.

12 oz.	cheese tortellini
1 (29 oz.) can	tomato sauce
1 (14.5 oz.) can	diced tomatoes
4	garlic cloves, minced
2 tsp.	salt
1 tsp.	black pepper
2 cups	chicken broth
1 (6 oz.) can	tomato paste
pinch	red pepper flakes (optional)
2 Tbsp.	sugar
4 cups	milk
1 cup	half-and-half
1 Tbsp.	dried basil

Garnish:

Parmesan cheese, shaved
fresh basil

Cook tortellini al dente in boiling, salted water. Remove from heat and drain immediately; set aside. Place tomato sauce, diced tomatoes, garlic, salt, and pepper in a large stockpot and simmer for 5 minutes. Add chicken broth, tomato paste, red pepper flakes, sugar, milk, half-and-half, basil, and cooked tortellini. Heat just until hot. Do not overheat, or half-and-half may curdle. Stir and serve. Garnish with shaved Parmesan and basil. Beware: you might like this soup so much you'll want to swim in it! Serves 6–8.

Homemade Beef, Chicken, or Vegetable Broth

Homemade broth adds an incredible amount of nutrition to your dish. I know it is so tempting to throw beef and poultry bones straight into the trash, but the gelatin that is produced from cooking them is very good for you. It really does not take a lot of work to make a good broth. Just throw everything into a big stockpot or slow cooker and let the simmering do its work.

16–20 cups	water
1 whole	chicken frame with some meat still on or 1 lb. of bone-in beef short ribs (omit for a vegetable broth)
1 lg.	onion
6	garlic cloves, whole
2 med.	carrots, quartered
2 stalks	celery, quartered
2 Tbsp.	vinegar
12 sprigs	fresh parsley (or 2 Tbsp. dried)
8	whole allspice (optional)
2	bay leaves
2 Tbsp.	salt
1 tsp.	pepper

In a large stockpot, place all ingredients and cook over medium-high heat. Just before the boiling point, reduce heat to low, cover, and simmer for 4–6 hours. It is best if you do not allow the mixture to boil. If your mixture boils, you will likely have a cloudy broth and scum will form on the top (if it does just scoop off and discard). Remove broth from heat and allow to cool completely. Strain and discard everything but the liquid. You can also cook on high in your slow cooker for 4–5 hours. You can store the broth in glass jars in the refrigerator for 2 months; it also freezes well. Yields 4 quarts.

    🐓 **And Another Thing . . . And Another Thing . . .** This recipe is particularly great if you have a sick person in your house because of the health benefits the bones add to your broth, such as essential minerals. Adding something acidic such as vinegar to your broth particularly draws out the calcium, magnesium, and potassium. Traditionally, broth you buy in the grocery store is made with meat pieces and vegetables only, no bones. Stock, however, has been cooked with the actual bones, not just meat. If you have options, always choose stock over broth and be sure to never throw bones away without first tossing them into a slow cooker and letting the slow cooker do the work for you to create a rich broth. Even just simmering water and bones will give you a great broth to have on hand.

Food for Thought

My father was a bi-vocational Mennonite pastor, so in addition to running the farm we opened our home to a lot of people. In my home growing up, everything shut down Saturday night in preparation for Sunday. Sunday was a special day for us. My father was very strict about what we were allowed to do. We joke about it now, but he instilled a principle in us that I want to pass on to my own children. In Mennonite culture, on Sunday you literally take a rest. It is such a positive thing for families, relationships, and the physical and spiritual well-being of a person. We ate a bang-up good meal after church Sunday morning; I am not sure it was rest for my mom, but it was a time for us to eat a wonderful lunch together and listen to *Adventures in Odyssey*! It was so fun to walk into the house after church and have those delicious smells hit you at the door. How do you prepare for your own day of rest, for your Sabbath? It's the time when the world stops and you rejuvenate. Maybe life has become frantic and too hectic. I encourage you to incorporate this principle of rest and see what it will do for your soul!

5

Garden Fresh Veggies,
Comfort Food, and Sides

I love cooking dishes with the colors of nature, and summer is the best time
of all to do that. If you have a little garden patch you can acquire every
color possible. It is so delightful to sit down to an arrangement of color
that comes from summer fare, whether it's fresh corn on the cob with peaches
for lunch or just-picked-from-the-garden salad for dinner. What inspires you
in the kitchen?

Brown Butter Green Beans

1 lb.	fresh green beans
½ cup	onion, diced
3 Tbsp.	salted butter (no substitutions)
1½ tsp.	salt, divided
½ tsp.	fresh cracked pepper

Place green beans in saucepan. Add 1 inch of water and 1 teaspoon salt. Bring to a boil. Boil for 7 minutes until crisp-tender. Drain.

In frying pan, heat butter over low heat until melted. Once butter is melted, add onions and cook for 5 minutes, then turn heat up to medium and cook for 2–3 minutes, until butter turns brown and fragrant. Remove from heat and pour over green beans. Sprinkle with remaining ½ teaspoon salt and pepper. Serve immediately. Yields 2–3 servings.

Roasted Asparagus

1 lb.	spring asparagus, washed and snapped
2 Tbsp.	olive oil
1 Tbsp.	balsamic vinegar
	salt and pepper to taste
2 Tbsp.	Parmesan cheese, fresh shaved

Preheat oven broiler. Place snapped asparagus on an ungreased baking sheet and sprinkle with oil, vinegar, salt, and pepper. Roast for 3–4 minutes, turn, and roast an additional 3–4 minutes.

Remove from oven, place in serving bowl, and sprinkle with Parmesan cheese. Serve immediately. Yields 2–3 servings.

Colorful Grilled Veggies

1 cup	cherry tomatoes, halved
1	green bell pepper, cut into chunks
1	sweet red pepper, cut into chunks
1 cup	fresh mushrooms, sliced
1 sm.	sweet or red onion, coarsely chopped
1 Tbsp.	apple cider vinegar
2 Tbsp.	olive oil
1 tsp.	lemon juice
1	garlic clove, minced
½ tsp.	dried basil (or 1 tsp. fresh)
½ tsp.	dried rosemary (or 1 tsp. fresh)
½ tsp.	dried parsley (or 1 tsp. fresh)
½ tsp.	salt
½ tsp.	fresh cracked pepper

Place all the veggies in a large piece of tinfoil. In a small bowl, combine the vinegar, oil, lemon juice, garlic, herbs, salt, and pepper. Drizzle over vegetables. Fold foil around vegetables and seal tightly. Grill over medium heat for 15–17 minutes or until vegetables are done to your liking. Serves 3–4.

🐌 **And Another Thing . . . And Another Thing . . .** You can also roast the vegetables in your oven instead of wrapping them in foil and grilling them. Set oven to 350°F and roast on a baking sheet for 25 minutes. Stir every 10–15 minutes.

Black Bean, Mango, and Tomato Salad

This is delightful served alongside rotisserie or grilled chicken.

⅓ cup	fresh lime juice
⅓ cup	water
⅓ cup	olive oil
1 Tbsp.	honey
1 tsp.	cumin
1 tsp.	salt
¼ tsp.	crushed red pepper (more or less for desired hotness)
2 lg.	mangoes, diced
2 (15 oz.) cans	black beans, drained and rinsed
2 cups	tomatoes, diced
½ cup	red onion, diced
⅓ cup	fresh cilantro, minced

In a small bowl stir together lime juice, water, oil, honey, cumin, salt, and red pepper. In another bowl mix together mango, beans, tomatoes, onion, and cilantro. Add dressing and stir to combine. Refrigerate for at least 2 hours. Serves 5–6.

I sometimes forget how blessed and rich with local products my family was. Our Amish neighbors provided us with all the fresh, free-range eggs we ever needed. My mom still gets her whole chickens from them. Fresh strawberries, fresh free-range turkey for Thanksgiving—the list goes on. We also had our own garden. Even though I have long been gone from the homestead, I still hear about it every year when my mother digs up those first red potatoes in late spring. Growing up, we could have all the farm-fresh milk our hearts could ever want. We raised our own beef and raspberries and made our own fresh grape juice; farmland is rich with so many good things! It really can be done. Sure it's hard work, but it is so rewarding and the memories I have of all those wonderful things are priceless.

Amish Fried Dressing

I learned to make a version of this when I worked at an Amish restaurant in Holmes County, Ohio. I was amazed at their dressing. I learned it was lightly pan-fried; no wonder all the guests raved about it. It comes as no surprise that I could eat this more than once a year! Dressing this moist should be at every family feast.

8 cups	bread cubes
½ cup	celery, chopped fine
½ cup	onion, chopped fine
½ cup	carrots, chopped fine
2 cups	chicken broth, divided
5	eggs
2½ cups	milk
½ tsp.	salt
½ tsp.	fresh cracked pepper
1 tsp.	poultry seasoning
¼ cup	dried parsley
4–6 Tbsp.	salted butter

Preheat oven to 325°F. Toast bread cubes on a cookie sheet for 15–20 minutes. While bread is toasting, combine celery, onion, carrots, and 1 cup chicken broth. Bring to a boil and boil for 5 minutes. Beat eggs; add milk, remaining chicken broth, salt, pepper, poultry seasoning, and parsley. Combine egg mixture with toasted bread and cooked vegetables.

Melt 2 tablespoons butter in a large frying pan, and pour in half of the bread mixture (mixture will be runny; reserve excess liquid). Fry lightly, then place in a lightly greased 9 x 13 dish. Repeat frying process with remaining bread mixture, adding more butter as needed. Pour any excess liquid over dressing and dot with remaining butter. Bake uncovered for 30–40 minutes. Serve with gravy (for an easy recipe, see Brown Beef Gravy on page 144). Serves 6–8.

Black Beans and Rice

I did not grow up eating a lot of beans and rice but I have come to enjoy this dish and many similar variations. I want to instill in my children an appreciation for foods from different cultures, not just the foods they are comfortable with. This is also an inexpensive meal. For me the key to this dish is the cumin; for my husband it is the fresh cilantro.

1 cup	onion, chopped
½ cup	green bell pepper, chopped
½ cup	red bell pepper, chopped
1 Tbsp.	jalapeño peppers, chopped (more or less to taste)
5	garlic cloves, minced
3 Tbsp.	olive oil
3 (15 oz.) cans	black beans, drained and rinsed
1 cup	chicken broth (1½ cups for stovetop version)
1 cup	tomato juice (1½ cups for stovetop version)
1 Tbsp.	chili powder
2 tsp.	cumin
1½ tsp.	salt
½ tsp.	pepper
3 cups	jasmine rice, cooked

Optional toppings:

cheddar cheese, shredded

tomatoes, diced

sour cream

fresh cilantro, chopped

green bell peppers, diced

jalapeño peppers, diced

black olives

Sauté onions, peppers, and garlic in olive oil for approximately 5 minutes. Remove from heat and place in slow cooker. Add beans, chicken broth, tomato juice, and seasonings. Cook on high for 3–4 hours. Serve beans over rice with desired toppings.

Stovetop version: In a large skillet, sauté onions, peppers, and garlic in olive oil for approximately 5 minutes. Add beans, chicken broth, tomato juice, and seasonings. Simmer uncovered for 35–45 minutes over medium heat. Serve beans over rice with desired toppings.

🐾 **And Another Thing . . . And Another Thing . . .** During late summer I purchase a quantity of peppers at the farmer's market and simply wash them, cut them, and freeze them in resealable freezer bags. I usually cut the peppers up several different ways, some for sautéing and some for pizzas. Peppers have a ridiculous price tag in the winter, but in late summer when farm markets are trying to get rid of the excess, they are much cheaper. It is a great way to save on your grocery bill in the winter months!

Mexican Spoon Corn Casserole

½ cup	salted butter, room temperature
2	eggs, slightly beaten
1 cup	plain yogurt or sour cream
1 (4 oz.) can	diced green chiles, drained
1 (15 oz.) can	cream style corn, undrained
1 (8.5 oz.) box	corn muffin mix
	red pepper flakes (optional)

Preheat oven to 350°F. Mix together butter, eggs, and yogurt. Add chiles, corn, corn muffin mix, and red pepper flakes. Pour into a greased 8 x 8 baking dish. Bake uncovered for 45 minutes. Serves 6.

🐾 **And Another Thing . . . And Another Thing . . .** This is great served with tacos or enchiladas! Place thin jalapeño rings on top before baking or stir in ¼ cup diced red pepper for a little color. When serving a Mexican meal, buy new 6- or 8-inch terra-cotta saucers (for flowerpots) to serve your cheese, lettuce, olives, and other toppings. It is a great way to jazz up a party without too much expense. The best part is you can use them for the next party too.

Baked Zucchini Noodles with Cheese and Herbs

In late summer, when you have picked and prepared more zucchini than you know what to do with, this simple side is a great way to add a fresh twist to your family's dinner.

1 lb. (4–6 sm.)	zucchini
¼ cup	olive oil
3	garlic cloves, minced
1 Tbsp.	fresh oregano, chopped (or 1 tsp. dried)
1 Tbsp.	fresh parsley, chopped (or 1 tsp. dried)
1 Tbsp.	fresh basil, chopped (or 1 tsp. dried)
	salt and pepper
1 cup	fresh tomatoes, diced
¼ cup	Parmesan cheese, grated
¼ cup	half-and-half

Preheat oven to 400°F. With a vegetable peeler, make long strokes down zucchini to get ¼-inch-wide zucchini noodles. Place in a large bowl. Drizzle with olive oil. Add garlic and herbs and toss noodles. Spread noodles onto 2 cookie sheets. Sprinkle with salt and pepper. Cover with foil and bake for 10–12 minutes. Place noodles in a serving bowl and toss with tomatoes, cheese, and half-and-half. Serve immediately. Serves 4.

Zucchini and Ricotta Bake

When I served this the first time I was unsure if it would be good. But it was a hit from the start, and has become a favorite. The added plus is the ease with which you can assemble this dish. Throw some chicken on the grill and you have a wonderful dinner to serve to your family without spending all afternoon in the kitchen. If you are attempting to watch calories or you don't have a piecrust on hand, this also is wonderful without a crust.

4 sm.	zucchini (2½ cups sliced, total)
¼ tsp.	fresh cracked pepper
1 Tbsp.	fresh dill weed (or 1 tsp. dried)
2	eggs, lightly beaten
1 cup	ricotta cheese
¼ cup	Parmesan cheese
¾ cup	mozzarella cheese, shredded
½ cup	half-and-half
1	piecrust, unbaked (optional)

Preheat oven to 350°F. Peel zucchini if skin is tough, and cut into half-dollar slivers. Mix zucchini, pepper, and dill together. Stir together eggs, ricotta, Parmesan, mozzarella, and half-and-half. Add zucchini mixture. Pour into piecrust and bake uncovered for 1 hour or until knife inserted in center comes out clean.

Creamy Baked Macaroni and Cheese

There was never any of this left when my mother made it. She always made it in a big yellow baking dish. If I could find one today, I would buy it out of pure nostalgia. I have vivid memories of my father scraping off the crusty sides even after the last morsel had been taken out. If my mom was out of milk, she would have one of my brothers run to the milk house to get some while my father was milking cows. Somehow, when we knew this dish was on the menu, it seemed easier to do the chores of feeding the calves, rabbits, dogs, cats, and pigs. As grown kids we all still love Mom's baked mac and cheese! This is a version of her creation. You can bake this in the oven or slow cooker. My mother always made it in the oven, and baking it in the oven gives it a crispy golden topping.

Slow cooker version:

3 Tbsp.	salted butter
2½ cups	macaroni, uncooked
1 tsp.	salt
¼ tsp.	pepper
½ cup	American cheese, diced
1 cup	Monterey or cheddar cheese, shredded
3 cups	milk

Melt butter and pour over macaroni. Add salt and pepper. Pour into slow cooker. Stir in cheese and pour milk over top. Cook on low for 4 hours. Serves 4–6.

Oven version:

3 Tbsp.	salted butter
2½ cups	macaroni, uncooked
1 tsp.	salt
¼ tsp.	pepper
½–¾ cup	American cheese, diced
1 cup	Monterey Jack or cheddar cheese, shredded
1	egg, slightly beaten
4 cups	milk

Preheat oven to 325°F. Melt butter and pour over macaroni in baking dish, tossing to coat. Add salt, pepper, cheese, and egg. Stir in milk. Bake uncovered for 90 minutes. Do not stir while baking. This comes out of the oven golden brown and creamy. Serves 4–5.

Campfire Potatoes

This is an all-time Falb family favorite we adopted when I was growing up. We used it when we went camping—and when we wished we were camping! There were many times we would start a campfire in our backyard on weekends and sit around it for hours. Often on Sunday nights after church we would invite the youth group over to sit around the campfire with us. Any cool summer night is the right night for a campfire. There are so many good conversations to be had, problems to be solved, songs to be sung, dreams to be born, and strengths to affirm around a fire. So whether you're preparing dinner to share around a fire or simply roasting marshmallows, don't miss the opportunity to enjoy the beauty of burning embers and the sweet fellowship that is born around those quiet moments. Your life will be richer for years to come.

4–6 lg.	redskin potatoes, thinly sliced (unpeeled)
1 sm.	onion, thinly sliced
2	garlic cloves, minced
2 Tbsp.	fresh parsley, minced (or 1 Tbsp. dried)
½ tsp.	salt
½ tsp.	fresh cracked pepper
2–3 Tbsp.	salted butter, thinly sliced
½ cup	cheddar cheese, shredded

Take an 18-inch piece of foil and arrange potato slices on half of it. Add onions, seasonings, butter, and cheese. Fold up into a pocket so that no heat can escape (potatoes will cook more rapidly). Bake in oven at 350°F for 30–45 minutes or grill for 20–22 minutes, until potatoes are tender. Yields 4 servings.

> And Another Thing . . . And Another Thing . . . To add a little flair you can serve with diced green onions, bacon pieces, and sour cream.

Garlic Mashed Potatoes

My mother makes the best mashed potatoes. The best—period. As hard as I try, my mashed potatoes never taste like hers, but it could be I just like it when all the work is already done and I can get right to the eating! My mother is the queen of garlic, and this delicious recipe uses quite a bit.

4 lbs.	white potatoes, peeled and quartered
1 tsp.	salt
8	garlic cloves, minced
½ cup	salted butter, diced
½ cup	milk (more or less)
1 tsp.	salt
½ tsp.	fresh cracked pepper
⅔ cup	plain Greek yogurt or sour cream
1–2 Tbsp.	fresh parsley (or 2 tsp. dried)

Boil potatoes, salt, and garlic together for approximately 45 minutes, until very soft. Drain potatoes completely and add remaining ingredients. Beat with an electric mixer until soft and smooth. Garnish with more parsley and butter. Serve immediately. Serves 7–8.

   And Another Thing . . . And Another Thing . . . A quick, easy, and more nutritional approach to this recipe is to wash the potatoes and quarter them without peeling. Cook and mash them with the skins on. I like to use redskin potatoes if I choose to do it this way. My mother says to always put 1 tablespoon of butter in your potatoes while they are boiling. It keeps the potatoes and water from boiling over. I started doing it and I think she is right, odd as it seems. It sure beats a messy, starchy potato-water stovetop.

Whipping Cream Potatoes

This is the simplest of all side dishes. It doesn't get any easier than this, and people always rave about this dish. They would rave even more if they really knew how little time it takes to prepare if you use frozen hashbrowns. This is another of my mother's favorite go-to recipes.

1 (30 oz.) bag	frozen hash browns (or 10 cups cooked, shredded potatoes)
1½ cups	whipping cream
2 tsp.	salt
½ tsp.	pepper

Preheat oven to 350°F. Beat whipping cream until soft peaks form (very important!). Fold hash browns into whipped cream; add salt and pepper. Pour into a 9 x 13 baking dish and bake uncovered for 60–70 minutes, until golden brown. Serves 7–8.

🐦 **And Another Thing . . . And Another Thing . . .** For variety, add 1 cup shredded cheddar cheese and/or 3 tablespoons fresh chives. Every time I make this dish, I never make enough. Somehow it always gets eaten all up. It's that good!

Old-Fashioned Potato Cakes

When making mashed potatoes for Sunday lunch be sure to make extra, and then one night that week you can easily make these yummy cakes to go with your meatloaf.

2 cups	mashed potatoes
1	egg, lightly beaten
⅛ tsp.	fresh cracked pepper
½ tsp.	salt (optional)
1 Tbsp.	flour
1 Tbsp.	minced onion
1½ tsp.	dried chives or parsley
1 Tbsp.	cream
2–4 Tbsp.	salted butter

Mix together potatoes, egg, pepper, salt, flour, onion, chives, and cream. Shape into 2-inch round cakes. Heat skillet over medium-high heat, melt 2 tablespoons salted butter in pan, and fry cakes approximately 3–4 minutes per side. Add more salted butter as needed. Serves 3–4.

Parmesan Italian Rice

This would be a great side dish for Golden Salmon Cakes (page 154) or baked chicken breasts topped with marinara sauce. I am always looking for ways I can pack nutritional greens into our diets. It can be a challenge but with this dish, it is subtle and tasty. I think even your kids will enjoy it.

2 cups	chicken broth
1 cup	jasmine or long grain rice
1 Tbsp.	olive oil
1	garlic clove, chopped
1 cup	fresh spinach, chopped fine
¼ tsp.	dried Italian seasoning
¼ cup	Parmesan cheese

In a medium saucepan, bring broth to a boil. Stir in rice, oil, and garlic. Reduce heat to low. Cover and cook for 20 minutes or until rice is tender. Stir in spinach and Italian seasoning. Let set for 5 minutes. Right before serving, stir in Parmesan cheese. Serves 3–4.

> *And Another Thing . . . And Another Thing . . .* You don't need to use jasmine rice to make this dish. Jasmine is just my all-time favorite. It's so good. If you start cooking with jasmine rice, you probably won't want to return to long or short grain ever again!

Fresh Tomatoes with Feta or Fresh Mozzarella

There's nothing really new or outrageous about this dish. What makes it extra special is fresh-picked tomatoes and basil from your own garden or locally grown ones from your farmer's market. This tops the chart on the barometer of EASIEST of all side dishes to prep.

5–6	fresh tomatoes
2 Tbsp.	olive oil
2 tsp.	balsamic vinegar
	fresh cracked pepper, to taste
	sea salt, to taste
10–12 leaves	fresh basil, chopped
4 oz.	feta, crumbled (or 8 oz. fresh mozzarella, sliced)

Slice tomatoes and lay half of them on a flat platter. Drizzle with half the oil and vinegar. Sprinkle with fresh pepper and salt, then half of the basil and cheese, if using feta. (If using mozzarella, I like to tuck the cheese under the tomatoes a bit.) Repeat layers, starting with tomatoes. Serves 10–12.

> *And Another Thing . . . And Another Thing . . .* A really nice presentation for this salad is to use tomatoes in a variety of colors and sizes. I like to use heirloom as well as roma tomatoes. Feta and mozzarella are two very distinct cheeses, but both pair well in this salad. Choose which one works best for your family.

Tomato Tart

This delicious buttery tart is the perfect complement to a cup of soup. If you use a tart pan instead of a traditional American pie plate, it will make your guests feel like they are eating at a French café. At the end of your meal, be sure to serve a good, strong cup of coffee with a spot of cream.

1 (9 in.)	piecrust, unbaked
1½ cups	mozzarella cheese, divided
4–6	roma tomatoes
¾ cup	fresh basil leaves, loosely packed
4	garlic cloves
2	eggs, beaten
2 Tbsp.	milk
¼ tsp.	fresh cracked pepper
1 cup	cottage cheese
¼ cup	Parmesan cheese, shredded
	sea salt, to taste

Preheat oven to 450°F. Press piecrust into tart or pie pan and trim the edge. Bake crust for 6 minutes. Remove from oven and sprinkle 1 cup of the mozzarella cheese in the bottom. Set aside. Reduce oven temperature to 375°F.

Cut tomatoes into thin slices. Drain on a paper towel. In a food processor, combine basil and garlic and pulse until coarsely ground, or mince by hand.

In a medium bowl, stir together basil mixture, remaining mozzarella cheese, eggs, milk, pepper, cottage cheese, and Parmesan cheese. Spread a thin layer of tomatoes over piecrust. Spread cheese mixture evenly on top, then add another layer of tomatoes. Sprinkle with coarse sea salt.

Bake for 25–30 minutes or until golden. Let stand for 10 minutes before cutting. Serve warm or cold. Serves 4–6.

🍵 **And Another Thing . . . And Another Thing . . .** If you have leftover tomatoes from your garden you cannot use fast enough, chop and freeze in 1- or 2-cup amounts in freezer bags, and next winter when a recipe calls for diced tomatoes, you'll have "your own" to put in the recipe. Immediately freezing fresh tomatoes from your garden allows you to retain their maximum nutritional value.

Yellow Squash Muffins

This is a great way to use up summer squash when they are in overabundance in late summer. I would never have made this recipe had I not tasted these. It sounds like an odd combination but is a great addition to a pasta dish or to a big summer salad.

4 cups	summer squash, cubed
1½ cups	water
3	eggs
1 cup	sugar
1 cup	plain yogurt or sour cream
½ cup	canola oil
2 tsp.	salt
2 tsp.	baking soda
3½ cups	flour

Preheat oven to 350°F. Place squash in a small saucepan. Add water to cover squash and cook over medium-high heat until very soft, approximately 20 minutes. Do not drain. When slightly cooled, purée squash in blender. Beat eggs well; add sugar, yogurt, oil, salt, baking soda, and flour and stir until well mixed. Stir in puréed squash. Bake in greased or lined muffin pan for 18–20 minutes or until toothpick inserted in center comes out clean. Yields 24 muffins.

Tomato Toppers

1 qt.	cherry tomatoes
8 oz.	cream cheese, softened
3 strips	bacon, cooked and crumbled
2 Tbsp.	green onions, minced
1 Tbsp.	fresh basil, minced
1 tsp.	Worcestershire sauce
¼ tsp.	fresh ground black pepper

Cut a thin slice off the top of each tomato. You may also want to cut a thin slice off the bottom of the tomato so it sits upright. With a grapefruit spoon, spoon out the pulp. Invert tomatoes on a paper towel to drain. Mix together cream cheese, bacon, green onions, basil, Worcestershire sauce, and black pepper. Fill tomatoes with cream cheese mixture using a little spoon. Sprinkle with fresh minced basil or parsley, if desired. Refrigerate until ready to serve. Arrange on a platter with lettuce for garnish.

🐦 **And Another Thing . . . And Another Thing . . .** These also make a very nice appetizer.

Food for Thought

I have a dear, sweet, godly mentor named Martha whom I don't get to connect with nearly as often as I would like. When she speaks, she speaks the very words of Jesus into my soul. Often after seeing her I stop and say to myself, *I had no idea I was that parched.* During a particularly hard time in our family, as I was baring my soul to her, she encouraged me to "struggle well." I had never heard of anything like that. It was a new thought, and it was freeing. *So struggle is good? And I'm allowed to question? Struggle is healthy? Struggle is okay?* I realized years later that to deny the struggle of life would stifle my heart. It would shut something down in me that shouldn't be shut down. Sometimes life is very messy, but the more I can struggle honestly about what's going on, the freer I am and the freer I become. What are the struggles that you have encountered? Are you struggling through them well? Run to Jesus with the question.

6

Main Entrées

We like to entertain with "everyone gets involved" kinds of parties. This idea is not really traditionally American but it has turned out to be so much fun for us whenever we host like this in our home. Rarely in American culture, and for sure not in Mennonite culture, do we invite guests into our home and still have most of the food prep to do. But I have learned the joy in doing this from my friend Cheryl. She lived in China and Thailand for seven years, pouring the love of Jesus into orphaned children, and while living there learned how to cook some amazing food. She has shown me how much fun it can be to host a party and have your guests get involved in all the chopping of fresh vegetables, meats, and fruit for the recipes that evening.

We have made some incredible memories by having all the guests in the kitchen with us. Usually there are more hands than counter space, but we get pretty creative. It's usually men and women alike helping to make the evening happen. We usually conclude the food tastes better when we have all taken part in getting it on the table. This is one more reminder to me that food is about more than physical nourishment; it's also about the sense of community that comes from working closely together and sharing life together. Try it sometime. Have your guests get involved. It is so much fun and makes hosting simple! You get to do the grocery shopping (that's the fun part) and they get to help with the rest!

Baked Rosemary Chicken

One day when I was talking food stuff with my sister-in-law Linda, she told me about a version of roasted chicken that she makes for her family. She said that this is one of their favorite Sunday lunches. I soon discovered why. When you walk into the house after being away and the aromas of garlic and rosemary hit you, you just want to immediately sit down and eat away.

1 (3–5 lb.)	roaster chicken
1 sm.	onion
1	apple
2 stalks	celery
½ cup	salted butter
¼ cup	fresh rosemary (or 2 Tbsp. dried)
8	garlic cloves, sliced thin (or minced)
1 Tbsp.	seasoned salt
½ tsp.	fresh cracked pepper
½ tsp.	paprika (preferably smoked)
½ cup	water

Preheat oven to 275°F. Place chicken in a baking dish. Chop onion, apple, and celery into large pieces and stuff inside the chicken cavity. Melt butter in a small saucepan; add rosemary, garlic, seasoned salt, pepper, and paprika. Heat through, then remove from heat and pour over top of chicken. Rinse saucepan with ½ cup water and pour water into the baking dish. Cover dish with foil and bake for 3–3½ hours. Serves 5–6.

Bacon, Mushroom, and Cheese Chicken

4	boneless, skinless chicken breasts
1 tsp.	dried basil (or 2 tsp. fresh)
1 tsp.	dried parsley (or 2 tsp. fresh)
1 tsp.	dried oregano (or 2 tsp. fresh)
1	garlic clove, minced
½ cup + 1 Tbsp.	olive oil, divided
¼ cup	balsamic vinegar
1 cup	mushrooms, sliced
½ cup	onion, chopped
8 slices	bacon
½ cup	Monterey Jack or cheddar cheese, shredded
1 Tbsp.	dried parsley (or 2 Tbsp. fresh, minced)

Place chicken breasts in a resealable plastic bag. Mix together basil, parsley, oregano, garlic, ½ cup olive oil, and vinegar. Pour marinade over chicken. Seal bag and refrigerate at least 4 hours or overnight.

Preheat oven broiler. Remove chicken breasts and discard marinade. Sauté mushrooms and onion in remaining 1 tablespoon olive oil; set aside. Wrap each chicken breast with 2 slices uncooked bacon and place on cookie sheet. Broil for 6 minutes. Turn chicken, then top each breast with 1–2 tablespoons of mushrooms and onions. Sprinkle with cheese and broil for 4 more minutes, or until center of chicken breast is no longer pink. Remove from oven. Sprinkle with parsley and serve. Serves 4.

Baked Chicken with Rice and Broccoli

I like this particular chicken and rice casserole because there are no processed foods in it, unlike most casseroles.

1½ cups	rice, uncooked
1 tsp.	salt
1 tsp.	celery seed
½ cup	onion, chopped
3 cups	broccoli florets
1 cup	fresh mushrooms, sliced (optional)
3 cups	chicken broth
4	bone-in chicken breasts
	salt and pepper
½ tsp.	paprika

Preheat oven to 350°F. Pour rice in bottom of greased 9 x 13 pan, and sprinkle with salt and celery seed. Stir onions, broccoli, and mushrooms into rice. Pour chicken broth evenly over rice mixture. Sprinkle chicken with salt and pepper, and place on top of rice. Sprinkle with paprika. Cover dish with foil and bake for 45 minutes. Remove foil and bake an additional 10–15 minutes. Serves 4.

And Another Thing . . . And Another Thing . . . My mother would use boneless, skinless chicken breasts, and in the last 15 minutes of baking she would put a slice of Muenster cheese on top of each breast and let it melt and get all bubbly. If you do use boneless, skinless chicken breasts, reduce total baking time to only 45 minutes or until rice is tender.

Presentation Ideas for Entertaining

My favorite entertaining piece is an old wooden door turned into a table with sawhorses. If you would see that old door standing against the wall in our basement, you would think that even the junkyard wouldn't want it. But lay it on top of two sawhorses, and you have just transformed that old door into a glorious serving buffet for your backyard picnic.

Also, little crocks were not made only to sit around with pretties in them—they were also made to display food. I have flowerpots that display food beautifully. We get bogged down by what we don't have to make something pretty. Learning to be creative with what we have transforms everyday items into wonderful serving dishes or party decor. Mason jars hold silverware beautifully; you don't need to buy expensive silverware holders or allow the silverware to just lay on the table. If you have some unique vintage jars, use those. Rarely does everything match when I host a party. I can be very random with my displays.

Do you have an old, empty wooden window box? Fill it with ice and put all your condiments in it, or serve your salads in smaller bowls and place them in the window box of ice.

Entertaining should be fun, and if you get bogged down because you can't do it "good enough," that is not the true heart of entertaining. To me the true heart of entertaining is ultimately offering myself and blessing the people I have chosen to serve by invitation. It's also offering part of your soul to the people in your sphere. Preparing food is such a labor of love. It is a servant act, and as women, we don't often view it as that simply because it is such a basic need. God has created us to live in community, and we experience that best when we host. Pray over your evening as you prepare your food. Pray that your family could bless all who are entering your home. Pray for the needs you don't even know about in your guests' lives; they will probably leave your home refreshed and not really understand why. When I bring the life of Jesus into the simple acts of preparing food and praying, something mysterious happens to my guests and to me! It's ultimately the sweet peace of Jesus wafting through our homes.

Chicken and Herb Dumplings

6 cups	chicken broth, divided
1 cup	carrots, diced
2 cups	potatoes, diced
½ cup	onion, diced
½ cup	celery, diced
2 cloves	garlic, minced
½ cup	salted butter
½ cup	flour
2 tsp.	raw or white sugar
1 tsp.	dried basil
½ tsp.	fresh cracked pepper
1 (10 oz.) bag	frozen peas
4 cups	cooked chicken, cubed

For dumplings:

2 cups	flour
4 tsp.	baking powder
½ tsp.	cream of tartar
2 tsp.	sugar
½ tsp.	salt
1 tsp.	dried basil
1 tsp.	dried oregano
½ cup	salted butter, melted
¾ cup	milk

Preheat oven to 350°F. In a medium saucepan bring 2 cups chicken broth to a boil, then add carrots, potatoes, onion, celery, and garlic and cook for 5–8 minutes, until vegetables are tender. In a large skillet, melt butter and then add flour, sugar, basil, and pepper, whisking to form a paste. Add remaining 4 cups chicken broth; cook until thickened, approximately 3–4 minutes. Add cooked vegetables (do not drain them), frozen peas, and chicken. Pour mixture into a 9 x 13 baking dish. To make dumplings, combine dry ingredients with a fork, then stir in butter and add milk, stirring just until moistened. Drop by small tablespoons onto casserole (16–18 dumplings). Bake uncovered for 30 minutes.

If the dumplings are not completely done, cover and bake for an additional 8–10 minutes. Serves 6–8.

Chicken and Cashews with Broccoli

This recipe is from my dear friend Cheryl. She has learned to cook some amazing food and this is one of the recipes she has shared with me. Everything is so fresh. To me there is nothing that spells healthy quite like dishes like this. So yum!

3 Tbsp.	olive oil
1½ cups	boneless chicken breast, sliced in thin strips
2 cups	broccoli florets
8	garlic cloves, minced
1½ cups	onion, roughly chopped
1	green bell pepper, roughly chopped
2	Thai chili peppers, minced (optional—makes this dish very spicy)
½ cup	chicken stock
4	spring onions with greens on, chopped
¾ cup	raw cashews, chopped
3–4 cups	cooked rice

Sauce:

¼ cup	oyster sauce
1 Tbsp.	soy sauce
2 tsp.	fish sauce (optional)
1 Tbsp.	raw or brown sugar

Combine all ingredients for sauce and set aside. Heat oil in a frying pan or wok over medium-high heat. Add chicken, broccoli, garlic, onion, bell pepper, and chili pepper, if using. Stir fry for 5–6 minutes. Add chicken stock. Stir. When chicken is fully cooked, add sauce and stir-fry briefly. Add spring onions and cashews. Serve immediately over rice. Yields 4–6 servings.

Chicken Curry

We have friends who have given their lives to the children of India. I never make this dish without thinking of them. It also reminds me to pray for them. While visiting in the States on one of their trips, they made us an authentic Indian meal. And in Indian fashion, we sat on the floor and ate our rice and curry with our fingers. There are so many ways to do many things, aren't there? This is a simple example and a great way to teach my children that life as we know it in America is not the only way to do life. I pray that my children can learn this and learn it well. I pray the Lord will give me courage to walk to a different beat, to see life through many different eyes, and to find ways, such as this dish, to creatively impart this to my children.

4	boneless chicken breasts, diced (or 4 cups cooked chicken)
1 cup	onion, diced
2 Tbsp.	olive oil
4	garlic cloves, minced
3 Tbsp.	curry powder
1 tsp.	ground ginger
1 tsp.	crushed red pepper flakes (more or less, to taste)
1 tsp.	salt
½ tsp.	pepper
1	bay leaf
2½ cups	chicken broth
1 (13.5 oz.) can	coconut milk
2 Tbsp.	fresh cilantro, chopped (optional)
6	green onions, diced (optional)
3 cups	cooked rice

Sauté chicken and onion in olive oil for 5 minutes (if using cooked chicken, you will only need to sauté the onion); add garlic, seasonings, and chicken broth. Bring to a boil. Reduce heat and simmer for 30 minutes. Add coconut milk and simmer for 5 more minutes. Remove from heat and take out bay leaf. Serve over rice, and sprinkle with cilantro and green onions, if desired. Serves 4–5.

🐦 **And Another Thing . . . And Another Thing . . .** This dish is great in the slow cooker. Toss everything except the coconut milk, green onions, and cilantro in the slow cooker and cook on low for 6–8 hours. Add coconut milk for the last 30 minutes. You don't even need to sauté the chicken and onion first.

Slow Cooker Teriyaki Chicken

4–5 pieces	bone-in chicken (approx. 3½ lbs.)
1 cup	crushed pineapple, undrained
½ cup	soy sauce
2 Tbsp.	brown sugar
2 Tbsp.	molasses
1 Tbsp.	fresh ginger, grated
2	garlic cloves, minced
¼ cup	green onions, chopped

Place chicken in slow cooker. Mix together pineapple, soy sauce, brown sugar, molasses, ginger, and garlic. Pour sauce over chicken and sprinkle green onions on top. Cook on high for 3–4 hours or low for 5–6 hours. Serves 3–4.

Chicken with Pecan Sauce

This makes a very simple dinner dish. Add a medley of cooked vegetables for a side and you're ready to gather at the table.

½ cup	pecan halves
¼ cup	salted butter, divided
1 tsp.	salt
½ tsp.	cracked pepper
⅛ tsp.	red pepper (optional)
½ tsp.	paprika
¼ cup + 1 Tbsp.	flour, divided
8	chicken tenderloins or 4 chicken breasts, flattened
1 Tbsp.	brown sugar
2 Tbsp.	cider vinegar
½ cup	chicken broth
½ tsp.	dried thyme

Over medium-low heat, sauté pecans and 2 tablespoons butter for 2–3 minutes or until pecans are toasted and smell fragrant. Remove from heat. Mix salt, peppers, paprika, and ¼ cup flour in a small, shallow bowl. Dredge chicken in mixture. Sauté in remaining butter for 3–4 minutes per side or until golden brown and fully cooked. Place cooked chicken on a plate, cover with pecans.

Return skillet to heat and add remaining flour, brown sugar, vinegar, and chicken broth. Cook about 3 minutes, stirring, until gravy thickens. Remove from heat and stir in thyme. Spoon over pecans and chicken. Serve immediately. Serves 4.

Moroccan Chicken Kebabs

This dish is rich in flavor. Yum!

1½ lbs.	boneless, skinless chicken breast, cubed
¾ cup	peach or apricot jam
2	garlic cloves, minced
1 Tbsp.	fresh ginger, grated
1 Tbsp.	fresh cilantro, minced
½ tsp.	cinnamon
½ tsp.	turmeric (optional)
½ tsp.	salt
1 med.	onion, cubed

Place chicken in a container to marinate. Mix together jam, garlic, ginger, cilantro, cinnamon, turmeric, and salt. Pour over chicken, seal container, and shake to coat. Refrigerate at least 4 hours or overnight. If using wooden skewers, soak in water for 30 minutes to prevent burning. Discard marinade and thread skewers with chicken and onion. Spray preheated grill with cooking spray. Grill 5 minutes on each side or until cooked through. Yields 6–8 skewers.

And Another Thing . . . And Another Thing . . . If you are in a hurry and don't have time to do skewers, just cut chicken in long strips or use tenderloins and follow marinating directions. Serve with rice or couscous.

Creamy Tomato Basil Chicken Bake

This dish is simply and delightfully delicious served over whole wheat pasta with pesto.

1 (14.5) oz. can	tomatoes, diced
⅓ cup	onion, minced
1 (6 oz.) can	tomato paste
½ cup	half-and-half
¼ cup	chicken broth
1 Tbsp.	dried basil (or 2 Tbsp. fresh)
4	garlic cloves, minced
1 Tbsp.	sugar
1 Tbsp.	fresh oregano (or 1½ tsp. dried)
½ tsp.	salt
½ tsp.	fresh cracked pepper
6	boneless, skinless chicken breasts
1½ cups	mozzarella cheese, shredded
¼ cup	fresh parsley (or 2 Tbsp. dried)
¼ cup	fresh basil (or 2 Tbsp. dried)

Preheat oven to 350°F. Mix together tomatoes, onion, tomato paste, half-and-half, broth, basil, garlic, sugar, oregano, salt, and pepper. Place chicken breasts in a 9 x 13 baking dish. Pour sauce over top. Bake for 25–30 minutes. Sprinkle with mozzarella cheese, parsley, and basil. Bake an additional 7–10 minutes. Do not overbake. Serves 6.

&❧ **And Another Thing . . . And Another Thing . . .** You can also add 2 cups of fresh spinach to the sauce.

Parmesan Chicken

My friend Michelle declares she can't cook because she didn't grow up Mennonite. But whenever I eat any of her food, it is always fabulous. This recipe is no exception. She is amazing, and has introduced me to some wonderfully delicious recipes!

6	boneless, skinless chicken breasts
1 Tbsp.	dried Italian seasoning
½ tsp.	fresh cracked pepper
1 cup	Parmesan cheese
½ cup	salted butter, melted

Preheat oven to 350°F. Trim and flatten chicken breasts. Place Italian seasoning, pepper, and Parmesan cheese in a shallow dish; dip each chicken breast in melted butter and then in cheese mixture. Place in a 9 x 13 pan and bake for 25–30 minutes. Serves 6.

And Another Thing . . . And Another Thing . . . This is a very nice entrée to serve with a pasta dish. Because it's so simple to prepare, it's great to serve to company. There are always those last-minute details that can make hosting a little hectic. Knowing your meat is savory and ready to go gives you peace of mind as you prepare those last-minute dishes.

Slow Cooker Thai Chicken

1 cup	coconut milk
¼ cup	peanut butter
2 Tbsp.	red curry paste (in the international aisle of your grocery store)
2 tsp.	ginger, grated
3	garlic cloves, minced
½ tsp.	salt
1½ lbs.	bone-in chicken
1	red bell pepper, cut into chunks
1 lg.	onion, cut into chunks
1 cup	frozen peas

Optional garnishes:

½ cup	fresh cilantro, minced
½ cup	crushed peanuts
	lime wedges

In a small bowl, combine coconut milk, peanut butter, curry paste, ginger, garlic, and salt. Place chicken pieces in a slow cooker; add red pepper and onion. Pour sauce over top. Cover and cook on low for 3–4 hours. Add peas 20 minutes before serving. Serve over rice with desired garnishes.

Roasted Chicken Sausage, Apples, and Potatoes

Apples add a subtle sweetness to this savory dish. The first time I made this dish we devoured it in its entirety. This dish is a perfect spring dish, especially if you have fresh spring potatoes, onions, and thyme in your garden. It takes only 5 minutes to assemble. It is my go-to dinner on a hurried day! I hope you find it as delightful as we do.

1 lb.	chicken sausage breakfast links
5 med.	potatoes, quartered
12	green onions (or 1 lg. white onion cut into wedges)
2 sm.	apples, cored and quartered
10 sprigs	fresh thyme (or 1 Tbsp. dried)
1 Tbsp.	olive oil
½ tsp.	salt
¼ tsp.	fresh cracked pepper

Preheat oven to 375°F. Remove greens from onions and halve remainder. Place sausage links, potatoes, onions, and apples in a roasting pan. Lay thyme on top, drizzle with olive oil, and sprinkle with salt and pepper. Cover and bake for 2 hours. Remove thyme sprigs before serving. Serves 4.

And Another Thing . . . And Another Thing . . . You can also cook in a slow cooker on low for 5–6 hours. You don't get that brown, roasted effect, but the flavor is through and through when you make this in the slow cooker.

Barbecued Meatballs

The key to this recipe is the sauce. I have made homemade sauces before, but this is my favorite—by far!

Sauce:

1 cup	ketchup
⅓ cup	brown sugar
¼ cup	honey
¼ cup	molasses
2 tsp.	prepared yellow mustard
2 tsp.	Worcestershire sauce
½ tsp.	liquid smoke
⅛ tsp.	pepper

In a small saucepan, combine all ingredients. Heat and bring to a boil. Remove from heat as soon as it boils. This sauce stores nicely in the refrigerator for 3–4 months. It is wonderful with grilled chicken too! Yields 2 cups.

Meatballs:

1½ lbs.	lean hamburger
1	egg
⅓ cup	bread crumbs or oatmeal
¼ cup	onion, diced
1	garlic clove, minced
1 tsp.	salt
¼ tsp.	pepper
¼ cup	sauce

Preheat oven to 350°F. In a bowl, combine all ingredients until well mixed. Using a small ice cream scoop, drop meatballs on a foil-lined cookie sheet (to make cleanup easier) side by side. Bake for 25–30 minutes. Once cool, you can freeze these meatballs in 1½ cups sauce and pull out in the future for an easy dinner. If serving immediately, place meatballs in baking dish, drizzle 1½ cups sauce over, and bake for 45–60 minutes at 300°F. You can also place meatballs and sauce in a slow cooker on high for 2–3 hours. Yields 12–15 meatballs.

🦀 **And Another Thing . . . And Another Thing . . .** These meatballs are wonderful as grilled burgers. Instead of forming into balls, just form into patties and grill. Baste the burgers with some sauce while grilling, but be sure to save some sauce for slathering generously over the burgers once they are cooked. Perfection!

Simple Chicken Cordon Bleu

I enjoy good food, but I am also realizing my limitations with small children at my feet—and I am learning that now is not a time in my life to stress over fancy meals. Here is a nice dish to make an event or dinner a little extra special without all the fuss.

4	boneless chicken breasts, trimmed and pounded
¼ lb.	Swiss cheese, sliced
¼ lb.	deli ham, sliced thin
1 can	mushroom soup (or a serving of Cream of Celery, Chicken, or Mushroom Soup, page 210)
½ cup	milk
¼ cup	bread crumbs
1 tsp.	paprika
2 Tbsp.	fresh parsley (or 1 Tbsp. dried)
¼ tsp.	fresh cracked pepper

Preheat oven to 350°F. Layer chicken breasts, Swiss cheese, and ham in order in a 9 x 13 pan. Mix mushroom soup and milk together. Pour over top of the meat. Sprinkle with bread crumbs, then sprinkle paprika, parsley, and pepper on top. Cover and bake for 35–40 minutes or until chicken is done. Do not overbake. Serves 4.

Jenelle's Meatloaf

For me, meatloaf can be one of those odd, dry beef dishes we throw together to form a dinner entrée. But in my opinion this recipe is an exception to the rule. My sister Jenelle, who is very gifted in the kitchen, came up with this version; the combination of meats makes for a moist loaf. She has a meat-and-potatoes kind of family, and this one has pleased them all. I think it's a keeper.

1 lb.	ground turkey
1 lb.	sage sausage
1 lb.	ground beef
1 cup	carrots, shredded
½ cup	onion, chopped
3	garlic cloves, minced
½ tsp.	salt
½ tsp.	black pepper
1 Tbsp.	Worcestershire sauce
1 cup	dry bread crumbs
2	eggs
2 cups	beef gravy (see Brown Beef Gravy, below)

Preheat oven to 350°F. Mix together all ingredients except gravy and shape into 2 loaves, using loaf pans. (You can freeze one and bake the other.) Bake for 60–90 minutes, until meat is no longer pink. Serve with 1 cup gravy poured over each loaf. Each loaf serves 4–6.

🍂 **And Another Thing . . . And Another Thing . . .** Mashed potatoes and gravy are a very nice pairing with this entrée; just make a little extra gravy for your potatoes. Or you can purchase prepared gravy to pour on top of the meatloaf.

Brown Beef Gravy

¼ cup	salted butter
¼ cup	flour
2 cups	beef broth

Heat butter in a skillet until well browned, then add flour, stirring constantly. Remove from heat and add beef broth slowly. Stir constantly to avoid lumps. Return gravy mixture to heat, and heat until smooth and bubbly, approximately 1–2 minutes.

Swedish Meatballs

Because of the gravy you make with this recipe, these meatballs are wonderful to serve with mashed potatoes.

30	precooked meatballs
2 Tbsp.	salted butter
2 Tbsp.	olive oil
¼ cup	flour
2	garlic cloves, minced
1 tsp.	salt
½ tsp.	fresh black pepper
pinch	nutmeg
pinch	paprika
2½ cups	chicken broth
½ cup	sour cream
3 Tbsp.	fresh parsley

Place meatballs in slow cooker. In a small skillet, melt butter and oil on low heat, then add flour and whisk to make a paste. Add garlic, salt, pepper, nutmeg, and paprika, then increase heat to medium and add chicken broth. Stir frequently and cook until thickened, about 4 minutes. Pour gravy over meatballs. Cover and cook on low for 3 hours. Right before serving, add sour cream and parsley to slow cooker. Serves 10.

    🐾 **And Another Thing . . . And Another Thing . . .** You may also use uncooked meatballs in this recipe. You will just need to adjust the baking time by adding 3 additional hours on low or 2 hours on high. For extra fun and flavor, use the base recipe of Jenelle's Meatloaf (page 144) for your meatballs.

Mini Cheddar Meatloaves

My brother Michael and his family operate an active, working dairy farm. They milk one hundred and thirty cows three times a day and own about one hundred more head of cattle. It makes me tired just writing about it, but needless to say Michael needs his meat and potatoes after a hard day's work. His wife Heather was not a meatloaf fan, but after trying many recipes she came up with this one and her whole family likes it. She said, "When I can't think of anything else to make, I know this will be a hit!"

1 lb.	ground beef
1	egg
1 cup	cheddar cheese, shredded
½ cup	oatmeal
½ cup	milk
¼ cup	onion, chopped
1 tsp.	salt
½ cup	ketchup
¼ cup	brown sugar
1 tsp.	prepared mustard

Preheat oven to 350°F. Mix together ground beef, egg, cheese, oatmeal, milk, onion, and salt. Shape into 8 mini loaves; place in a greased 9 x 13 pan. In a small bowl combine ketchup, brown sugar, and mustard; spoon evenly over loaves. Bake uncovered for 45 minutes or until meat is no longer pink. Serves 4–5.

🐦 **And Another Thing . . . And Another Thing . . .** For a recipe like meatloaf, adding some oatmeal and cutting back on the amount of beef is a great way to add whole grain to a dish and also use less meat!

Pizza Hot Dish

1 lb.	ground turkey or beef
½ cup	onion, chopped
½ cup	green bell pepper, chopped
2 cups	pizza or pasta sauce
2	garlic cloves, minced
1 tsp.	dried oregano
1 tsp.	dried basil
½ tsp.	salt
¼ tsp.	fresh cracked black pepper
½ cup	fresh mushrooms, sliced
3 cups	whole wheat pasta of choice, cooked
2 Tbsp.	Parmesan cheese
2 cups	mozzarella cheese, shredded

Preheat oven to 350°F. Brown meat in a large skillet, add onions and green pepper, and sauté for 5 minutes. Add sauce, garlic, oregano, basil, salt, pepper, and mushrooms. Place cooked pasta in the bottom of a 9 x 13 dish. Pour meat sauce over and sprinkle both cheeses on top. Cover with foil. Bake for 35–45 minutes or until completely heated through. Serves 6–8.

ᕲ **And Another Thing . . . And Another Thing . . .** This dish is a great approach to pizza without all the calories.

Upside Down Pizza

For some reason, making pizza seems like a chore to me, but if I am hungry for something similar this is excellent. It's quick—which is what I need sometimes.

1 lb.	ground sausage or turkey sausage
1 lb.	hamburger
1 tsp.	garlic, minced
½ cup	red or green bell pepper, diced
1 cup	onion, diced
1 cup	mushrooms, diced
½ cup	pepperoni
32 oz.	pizza or pasta sauce
1 Tbsp.	fresh basil, chopped (or 1½ tsp. dried)
1 Tbsp.	fresh oregano (or 1½ tsp. dried)
3 cups	mozzarella cheese, shredded
1 (8oz.) pkg.	crescent rolls
⅓ cup	Parmesan cheese, shredded
2 tsp.	dried Italian seasoning

Preheat oven to 350°F. Place sausage and hamburger in a large stockpot. Add garlic, bell pepper, and onion. Sauté until meat is no longer pink and vegetables are cooked. Add mushrooms, pepperoni, sauce, basil, and oregano. Simmer for 5 minutes. Place in a 9 x 13 pan. Top with mozzarella cheese. Place flattened crescent rolls on top, pinching seams to seal. Sprinkle with Parmesan cheese and Italian seasoning. Bake for 30–35 minutes or until bubbly. Serves 8–10.

 And Another Thing . . . And Another Thing . . . I like to add 2 cups of fresh spinach to the meat mixture. It's a great way to get added nutrition in this dish.

Cheeseburger Quiche

I could eat quiche once a week. Somewhere along this journey of life, quiche has become one of my favorite foods. I think I was first introduced to it at a brunch as a little girl, but maybe it became my favorite food one gorgeous fall day when my friends and I were sitting outside a little café in France, or maybe it was a birthday party in the park one September day as the sun was setting to celebrate deep friendship. This food embodies so much more to me than just physical nourishment!

1 (9 in.)	extra deep piecrust, unbaked
½ lb.	ground beef
2	plum tomatoes, chopped
½ cup	onion, chopped
¼ cup	red bell pepper, chopped
2	garlic cloves, minced
½ cup	bacon, cooked and chopped
1 cup	cheddar cheese, shredded
4	eggs
1 cup	half-and-half
1 tsp.	salt
¼–½ tsp.	hot pepper sauce or crushed red pepper (optional)
½ tsp.	fresh cracked pepper
½ tsp.	garlic powder
1 Tbsp.	dried parsley
¼ cup	Parmesan cheese

Preheat oven to 350°F. Brown ground beef then add tomatoes, onion, red pepper, and garlic. Cook briefly. Transfer to piecrust. Sprinkle bacon and cheddar cheese over top of hamburger mixture. In another bowl beat eggs and add remaining ingredients. Pour over hamburger mixture. Bake for 50–60 minutes or until a knife inserted in center comes out clean. Let stand for 10 minutes before cutting. Garnish with extra bacon, diced tomatoes, shredded cheddar cheese, and parsley, if desired. Serves 4–6.

And Another Thing . . . And Another Thing . . . This is a nice dish to serve for a luncheon. Add a simple salad of mixed greens with strawberries, almonds, and a poppy seed dressing (such as Orange Poppy Seed Dressing, pg. 86). Or add a simple, special touch to the close of a summer meal with fruit kebabs. A short skewer threaded with melon balls, grapes, and/or strawberries and kiwi is simply beautiful.

Slow Cooker Lasagna

This entrée is very easy to make ahead of company coming, or simply if you have a busy couple of days ahead. You can get the ingredients prepped and then quickly assemble in your slow cooker the day it's needed. Yeah! While the spinach is optional, it is a fabulous way to add the nutritional value of this super food to this dish. And more than likely, your family will not even know they are eating spinach.

1 lb.	ground beef or turkey
½ cup	onion, chopped
2	garlic cloves, chopped
½ tsp.	salt
32 oz.	pasta sauce
16 oz.	ricotta cheese
2 cups	mozzarella cheese, shredded and divided
½ cup	Parmesan cheese, grated or shredded
1	egg
1 (10 oz.) pkg.	frozen chopped spinach, thawed and drained (optional)
¼ cup	fresh parsley, chopped (or 2 Tbsp. dried)
2 Tbsp.	fresh basil, chopped (or 1 Tbsp. dried)
½ tsp.	fresh cracked black pepper
6–8	lasagna noodles, uncooked

Brown ground beef and onions with garlic and salt. Add pasta sauce to meat mixture. In a separate bowl, mix together ricotta cheese, 1½ cups mozzarella cheese, Parmesan cheese, egg, spinach, parsley, basil, and pepper. Spread a thin layer of meat mixture in bottom of greased slow cooker and add a layer of lasagna noodles, breaking them as needed to fit, then add a layer of cheese mixture; repeat layers until beef and cheese mixtures are used up. Cook on low for 4 hours. Right before serving, sprinkle with remaining mozzarella cheese. Serves 8–10.

Slow Cooker Beef Tips with Mushrooms and Onions

2–3 cups	fresh mushrooms, washed and sliced
1 cup	onion, julienned
3 whole	garlic cloves
½ cup	flour
2 lbs.	stew beef tips
¼ cup	salted butter
1 cup	beef broth
2 tsp.	brown sugar
1 tsp.	chili powder
1 tsp.	salt
½ tsp.	black pepper

Place mushrooms and onions in the bottom of a slow cooker, then add whole garlic cloves. Place flour in a resealable plastic bag, add beef tips, and shake to coat. Brown butter in a skillet; add beef tips and cook for 3–4 minutes. Remove from heat and place beef on top of vegetables. Combine beef broth, brown sugar, chili powder, salt, and pepper and pour over beef. Cook on high for 2 hours, then reduce to low and cook for 3–4 more hours. Stir once. Serves 4–5.

And Another Thing . . . And Another Thing . . . Serve over buttered parsley egg noodles. Add ¼ cup salted butter and 2 tablespoons dried parsley to every 1 lb. of noodles you cook. Do a double batch of beef tips if your slow cooker allows, and you can freeze the leftovers for another night a month from now. The work will be mostly done, and you will be happy you did it.

Slow Cooker Pot Roast with Yukon and Sweet Potatoes

We grew up eating a lot of beef raised right on our farm. We ate more meals of beef and Amish egg noodles than I can count. However, the first time I made it for my husband, I clearly understood that he was not nearly as fond of that dish as I was. I concluded it would just have to be a dish I asked my mom to make for me when I visited her kitchen. Fortunately, we enjoy beef roasts prepared all different ways. Here is one of many versions of roasts that I make for my family.

3–4 lbs.	beef chuck roast
3 Tbsp.	oil or salted butter
2 med.	onions, thinly sliced
3 med.	baking potatoes, peeled and quartered
3 med.	sweet potatoes, peeled and quartered
1 cup	beef broth
1 tsp.	celery seed
2 tsp.	dried oregano
½ tsp.	dried rosemary, crushed
¼ tsp.	cinnamon
1 tsp.	salt
½ tsp.	fresh cracked pepper
1 cup	frozen peas

Heat oil or butter in a skillet over medium-high heat, sprinkle all sides of roast with salt, then brown roast for 3–4 minutes per side. Place roast in slow cooker and top with onions and potatoes. Combine broth with celery seed, oregano, rosemary, cinnamon, salt, and pepper. Pour over roast. Cover and cook on low for 8–9 hours. Add peas 1 hour before finished. Serves 6.

   And Another Thing . . . And Another Thing . . . In my experience, the slower and longer I can cook a roast, especially a less expensive cut of meat, the happier I am with the results. I never seem to have great success when I cook them on high heat.

Baked Ham with Brown Sugar Glaze

¾ cup   brown sugar, packed
¾ cup   honey
½ cup   Dijon mustard
¼ cup   apple juice
1 tsp.   whole cloves
1 (6–7 lb.)   ham

Mix together brown sugar, honey, mustard, apple juice, and cloves. Trim fat from ham and place in a slow cooker or baking dish. Baste ham with glaze mixture. Cover and bake according to directions on package.

Ginger and Honey Salmon

This is one of my favorite dishes!

⅓ cup   soy sauce
¼ cup   pineapple juice
¼ cup   honey
¼ cup   olive oil
1 Tbsp.   brown sugar
2   green onions, chopped
2   garlic cloves, minced
2 tsp.   fresh ginger, minced (or 1 tsp. ground ginger)
4   salmon fillets
2 Tbsp.   sesame seeds (optional)

Combine soy sauce, pineapple juice, honey, oil, and brown sugar. Add green onions, garlic, and ginger. Marinate salmon in ⅔ cup of mixture for 30 minutes or more. Drain and discard marinade. Preheat oven broiler. Place fillets in a baking dish; pour remaining marinade over fillets. Broil for 7 minutes, then add sesame seeds, if using, and broil 3–5 more minutes or until fillets flake easily. Serves 4.

Golden Salmon Cakes

There is something about canned meat that could promptly make me decide to eat only fruits, vegetables, and nuts. I don't know why I feel that way, but I do believe in the health benefits of salmon and want to get it into my family's diet as often as possible. This is a less expensive way to do that—and a really tasty dish! Parmesan Italian Rice (page 122) is an excellent side to serve with this dish.

2 (6 oz.) cans	wild salmon, drained and flaked
½ cup	bread crumbs or cracker crumbs
¼ cup	milk
2	green onions, thinly sliced (or ⅓ cup onion, minced)
2 Tbsp.	fresh parsley (or 1 Tbsp. dried)
2 Tbsp.	mayonnaise
2	garlic cloves, minced
2	eggs, slightly beaten
1 Tbsp.	soy sauce
1 tsp.	lemon juice
1 tsp.	paprika
½ tsp.	celery salt
¼ tsp.	fresh cracked pepper
⅛ tsp.	cayenne pepper
2 Tbsp.	salted butter
2 Tbsp.	olive oil

Combine all ingredients except butter and olive oil; form into 8 patties. Place butter and oil in a frying pan over medium-high heat and fry each patty for approximately 4 minutes per side, until golden. Makes 8 patties.

🐾 **And Another Thing . . . And Another Thing . . .** You can also broil these salmon cakes. Lightly brush with olive oil and broil for 5 minutes, then flip and broil an additional 3–4 minutes.

Grilled Tilapia with Mango Salsa

1 cup	mango, diced
1 cup	fresh pineapple, cubed
1 cup	tomato, diced
2	green onions, chopped
¼ cup	green bell pepper, minced fine
¼ cup	fresh cilantro, minced (or 2 Tbsp. dried)
pinch	red pepper flakes
3 Tbsp.	lime juice, divided
½ tsp.	salt, divided
1 Tbsp.	olive oil
¼ tsp.	ground white pepper
8 (4 oz.)	tilapia fillets

In a small bowl, combine mango, pineapple, tomato, green onion, green bell pepper, cilantro, red pepper flakes, 1 tablespoon lime juice, and ¼ teaspoon salt. Set aside.

Combine oil, white pepper, remaining salt, and remaining lime juice; brush over fillets. Coat grill rack with cooking spray before starting the grill. Grill fish uncovered over medium heat for 3–4 minutes per side, or until flaky. You can also broil fish on high for 10–12 minutes. Spoon salsa over fish fillets and serve immediately. Serves 5–6.

And Another Thing . . . And Another Thing . . . Green onions make a great garnish. Take a green onion and cut 1 inch from the top, and also cut off the tail from the bottom. Gently pull the green tops apart, toward the white of the onion. Submerge in cold water for 5 minutes. The greens will curl. This is a simple little addition to a plate, but it looks really pretty.

Shrimp on Rosemary Skewers

If you have fresh rosemary growing in your herb garden, it makes for some creative skewers. Serve this dish as an appetizer or main entrée at your next backyard picnic. My brothers, sister, and I all happened to be in Ohio on June 9 (which is our parents' anniversary) recently, so we all cooked up a dinner for our parents and allowed the grandkids to serve them out in their grapevine "Oasis." This was the appetizer. It's so fun to cook with my family.

8	fresh, strong rosemary sprigs, about 6 inches long
1 lb.	shrimp, uncooked
½ cup	peach preserves or jam
½ cup	flaked coconut
¼ tsp.	crushed red pepper
¼ tsp.	rosemary, minced

Wash rosemary springs and remove ¾ of the rosemary leaves, starting from the base of the stem, to create skewers. Thread shrimp on skewers. Mix together peach preserves, coconut, crushed red pepper, and rosemary. Brush on shrimp. Heat grill to medium-high and cook shrimp for 3–4 minutes per side or until opaque. Remove and serve immediately. Makes 8 skewers.

Almond Crusted Tilapia

4	tilapia fillets
	salt and pepper, to taste
2 Tbsp.	salted butter or Herbal Butter, melted (see recipe on page 209)
¼ cup	almonds, sliced
2 Tbsp.	bread crumbs
¼ cup	Parmesan cheese
2 Tbsp.	olive oil

Preheat oven to 375°F. Place tilapia fillets in a baking dish and sprinkle with salt and pepper. Drizzle melted butter over fillets. In a small bowl, mix together almonds, bread crumbs, and Parmesan cheese. Spread on top of fish. Drizzle with olive oil. Bake for approximately 10–12 minutes or until fish is opaque. Do not overbake.

Layered Meatless Mexican Casserole

Amanda made a similar version of this for our small group one night and it was a hit. Even my little boys ate it. When I find something they eat well, I want to make it every other night! This has such good flavor. If you want to add meat, simply brown a pound of ground beef and layer it between the refried beans and spinach. I am so happy to have found a Mexican dish that is not loaded with sour cream or flour tortillas (though I thoroughly enjoy both of those!) and is still packed with so much flavor.

6 cups	brown rice, cooked
1½ cups	salsa
1 tsp.	cumin
1 (15 oz.) can	refried beans
1 Tbsp.	chili powder
12 oz.	frozen corn
½ cup	green bell pepper, diced
½ cup	onion, diced
1 (10 oz.) pkg.	frozen spinach, thawed and drained
2 cups	cheddar cheese, shredded
	fresh cilantro (optional)

Preheat oven to 400°F. Combine cooked rice, salsa, and cumin. Set aside. Mix refried beans, chili powder, corn, green pepper, and onion together; set aside. In a greased 9 x 13 baking dish, place half the rice mixture on the bottom, then spread refried bean mixture over. Sprinkle spinach on top, then add remaining rice mixture. Cover with foil and bake for 25 minutes. Remove foil, add cheese, and bake for 5–7 minutes longer. Right before serving, sprinkle cilantro on top, if desired. Serves 8–10.

🕊 **And Another Thing . . . And Another Thing . . .** Chips and salsa complement this dish beautifully!

Food for Thought

Who feeds you? I don't mean who is feeding you physically, but rather who feeds your soul? What do you allow to filter in and out of your thoughts on any given day? Are these influences pointing you to Jesus? Are there people who encourage you along this journey called life, or are you allowing the influences of the world to squeeze the life out of you? There will always be this tug-of-war in our minds: the voice of the world versus the voice of Scripture. As followers of Jesus, we need to learn to think biblically and set our minds on the things that are positive, to think like Jesus thinks, and to focus on things that build our character instead of being consumed by culture. Here's a verse I like to call to mind, one that feeds my soul:

> Live in peace with each other. And we urge you, brothers and sisters, warn those who are idle and disruptive, encourage the disheartened, help the weak, be patient with everyone. . . . Rejoice always, pray continually, give thanks in all circumstances; for this is God's will for you in Christ Jesus. (1 Thess. 5:13–18 NIV)

7

Desserts

The LORD is my portion, saith my soul; therefore will I hope in him.

Lamentations 3:24 KJV

I was closing my Bible one morning after my quiet time, and mentally preparing for all that was ahead of me that weekend. I was cooking for multiple church-related events, hosting guests all weekend, and cooking Sunday lunch for forty. As I closed my Bible in that quiet moment, Proverbs 14:1 came to mind and I pondered the phrase, "The wise woman builds her house." What did that mean to me this particular day? My house was already built. It was clearly as if the Lord was saying, *Dawn, your physical dwelling is already built—but what are ways you can build on what is already constructed? Add little extra touches of my love. Your energy will be spent but the Lord is your portion—offer yourself. That is "building your household."*

As the woman of your domain, your story is going to look different from mine, but in what ways is God asking you to build your household today, and how are you hoping in him? It's more than just constructing the roof—it's about ways to build our hearts and our capacity to love in response to the people we call family and friends.

Chocolate Cream Pie

My husband's favorite dessert is chocolate cream pie. His mother always made it for him when we visited her in Florida. In March 2011, she passed on and went home to be with Jesus. I know her passing will make him even fonder of chocolate cream pie in the years to come.

1 (9 in.)	piecrust
¾ cup	white or raw sugar
¼ tsp.	salt
5 Tbsp.	cornstarch
3 Tbsp.	cocoa powder
2¼ cups	milk
3	egg yolks, well beaten
1 Tbsp.	salted butter
2 cups	whipping cream
⅓ cup	powdered sugar
1 tsp.	vanilla extract

Prick piecrust with a fork to prevent air pockets, then bake at 400°F for 10–12 minutes until golden. In a heavy saucepan, combine sugar, salt, cornstarch, and cocoa powder, and whisk well. Add milk and stir thoroughly. Heat saucepan on medium-low heat. Stir often, so mixture will not scorch or get lumpy. Once mixture has thickened or is starting to boil, cook 2 more minutes on low heat. Remove from heat. Take ¼ cup of hot, cooked custard mixture and add it to egg yolks; stir thoroughly. Add egg mixture to hot custard mixture and stir vigorously. Cook over low heat for 2 minutes, stirring constantly. Remove from heat and stir in butter.

Empty hot custard into a bowl and place a piece of plastic wrap directly on top of the custard so that it doesn't form a thick, crusty top layer; refrigerate and chill completely.

When ready to assemble pie, beat whipping cream until soft peaks form, then add powdered sugar and vanilla. Set aside 1½ cups of whipped cream. Mix chilled chocolate custard with remaining whipped cream. If the mixture is lumpy at first, continue beating until it is smooth, then pour into piecrust. Top with reserved 1½ cups whipped cream. Sprinkle mini chocolate chips on top of the whipped cream, if desired. Yields 6–8 pieces.

🐦 **And Another Thing . . . And Another Thing . . .** This is not hard to make, but it is very important to follow all of the steps, or you may end up with a pie that does not have a smooth texture.

Butterfinger Dessert

My mother used to make this *often*! I can still see my brother sitting down with a serving that was twice the amount anyone should eat; it brings a smile to my face and reminds me of happy times around the farmhouse table. This is such a simple recipe. You can whip it up in no time for a nice ending to a delicious meal for your family or your guests.

1½ cups	Ritz or Townhouse crackers, crushed
¼ cup	salted butter, melted
1 (5.1 oz.) box	instant vanilla pudding
2½ cups	milk
1.5 qts.	vanilla ice cream, softened (vanilla bean is my favorite)
1½ cups	whipping cream
⅓ cup	powdered sugar
3	Butterfinger candy bars (regular size)

Crush crackers and pour melted butter over them. Stir to coat evenly and press into the bottom of a 9 x 13 pan. Mix vanilla pudding and milk, then stir in ice cream. Pour over the cracker crust and refrigerate for 30 minutes. While that is setting up, beat whipping cream until soft peaks form. Stir in powdered sugar. Once pudding mixture is set, spread whipped cream on top. Crush candy bars and sprinkle on top of whipped cream. Chill for 2 hours. Serves 12.

Rhubarb Cream Pie

This is an excellent pie! My mother had rhubarb growing in her garden every spring. Rhubarb to me is an odd sort of fruit. How can it be good for you if you have to add so much sugar to make it edible? When I was six, my father gave me my heart's desire: two baby bunnies. I was so proud of them, I wanted them to have the best food. I would save every vegetable green we had, sneak carrots to take to them, and even take them fresh cut grass. One day in my attempt to feed my bunnies something other than grain pellets, I found the perfect thing: the large, green rhubarb tops. I proudly fed them the lush greens—but to my dismay they both died by the next morning. Rhubarb leaves are very poisonous. It was a very sad day to this little six-year-old. My father did replace the bunnies, and you can imagine my new bunnies never, ever got rhubarb leaves again. I was now happy and content to serve them only carrots and fresh spring lettuce.

1 (9 in.)	extra deep piecrust, unbaked
5–6 cups	fresh rhubarb, diced (or frozen, thawed, and drained)
3	egg yolks
¾ cup	half-and-half
1 cup	raw or white sugar
¼ cup	flour
½ tsp.	salt

Meringue:

4	egg whites
¼ tsp.	cream of tartar
½ tsp.	vanilla extract
6 Tbsp.	raw or white sugar

Preheat oven to 400°F. Place rhubarb in piecrust. In a small bowl, beat egg yolks until light and fluffy. Blend in half-and-half. Add sugar, flour, and salt; mix well. Pour over rhubarb. Bake for 10 minutes. Reduce oven temperature to 350°F and bake an additional 40 minutes.

For meringue, beat egg whites until soft peaks form. Add cream of tartar, vanilla, and half of the sugar. Beat again, then add remaining sugar. Spread over hot pie filling. Bake for 12–15 minutes or until lightly browned. Serves 6–8.

Chocolate Mocha Cream Puff

½ cup	salted butter
1 cup	boiling water
1 cup	white wheat flour (or all-purpose flour)
½ tsp.	salt
4	eggs, beaten
2 Tbsp.	instant coffee granules
1 Tbsp.	hot water
2 cups	heavy whipping cream
2 Tbsp.	powdered sugar
8 oz.	cream cheese, softened
1 (5.1 oz.) pkg.	instant chocolate pudding
1½ cups	milk
1 (14 oz.) can	sweetened condensed milk
¼ cup	chocolate syrup

Preheat oven to 350°F. For dough, melt butter in boiling water. Add flour and salt, and stir well. Add eggs gradually. Mixture will be runny. Spread into a greased 9 x 13 pan. Bake for 25–30 minutes. Cool.

For pudding, combine instant coffee and hot water; stir until dissolved. In another bowl beat whipping cream until stiff peaks form. Remove 1 cup of the whipped cream and stir in powdered sugar, making sure the whipped cream is still stiff. Set aside. In a separate bowl beat cream cheese until smooth; add pudding and milk and beat thoroughly. Add sweetened condensed milk and coffee mixture. Stir until well blended. Fold in unsweetened whipped cream. Place pudding mixture on top of cooled dough. Spread sweetened whipped cream over pudding mixture and drizzle with chocolate syrup. Serves 12–14.

🐦 **And Another Thing . . . And Another Thing . . .** This dessert is wonderful even without the coffee, so for the people in your life who don't like coffee desserts you can easily make this to please their palate.

Caramel Pear Crumble

My dear friend Emily made this dish one of the first times I was in her home. This recipe is a keeper, and reminds me of the beginning of a budding friendship. I am very nostalgic that way; when someone loves me well, the food they served me is tied into that love. There is something about a recipe from a kindred friend that makes the recipe even better. Think about who your kindred friends are and what food sounds good to you simply because there is no one who can make it quite like your friend does.

1¼ cups	all-purpose flour
1 cup	oatmeal
1 cup	brown sugar, packed
1 tsp.	cinnamon
½ cup	salted butter, softened
2 Tbsp.	milk
6–7	fresh pears, cored, peeled, and halved (or 2–15 oz. cans pear halves, drained)
12–15	caramels, unwrapped

Garnish:

whipped cream

cinnamon

Preheat oven to 350°F. In a medium bowl combine flour, oatmeal, brown sugar, and cinnamon. Stir in butter and milk; mixture will be crumbly. Set aside 1 cup. Press the remaining mixture into a greased 9 x 13 baking dish. Lay the pear halves on top of crumb mixture, core side up. Place 1 caramel in center cavity of each pear. Sprinkle reserved crumb topping over pears. Bake for 30–35 minutes or until pears are tender and top of dessert is golden brown. Serves 6–8.

Peach Cobbler

Buttery, sugar-laced, biscuit-like crumbles top this yummy bowl of peaches. Throw in a few blackberries if you were just out picking, and you have a perfect sweet! Peach cobbler and grilled chicken was another summertime meal on the farm. We would come in late from doing chores, baling hay, filling the silo, or working in the garden, and this is what we would eat. Not necessarily the most well-balanced meal, but it still evokes such good memories of coming in ravenously hungry and sharing tasty food with the ones I love. Yum!

4 cups	peaches, peeled and sliced
1 cup	blackberries (optional)
1 tsp.	cinnamon
⅔ cup	raw or white sugar
3 Tbsp.	salted butter, softened
1 cup	flour
1 tsp.	baking powder
⅓ cup	milk
2 Tbsp.	brown sugar

Preheat oven to 350°F. In a 9 x 9 ungreased baking dish, place fruit and sprinkle with cinnamon; set aside. With a hand mixer, beat sugar, butter, flour, baking powder, and milk together; crumble mixture over fruit. Sprinkle brown sugar on top. Bake for 45–55 minutes. Serve warm with vanilla ice cream. Serves 4–6.

Cherry Delight

My mother has taken a version of this dish to multiple potlucks and carry-in meals. She hasn't used a written recipe in years; it's one that's second nature to her. I never thought it was really that great until we no longer lived in the same state—and then I would get hungry for it! Funny how those things happen.

1½ cups	graham cracker crumbs
⅓ cup	salted butter, melted
2 Tbsp.	sugar
1 (1.4 oz.) box	lemon gelatin
1 cup	boiling water
1½ cups	whipping cream
¼ cup	powdered sugar
24 oz.	cream cheese, softened
¾ cup	raw or white sugar
1 (21 oz.) can	cherry pie filling
2 cups	frozen mixed berries, thawed and drained (or fresh strawberries)

Preheat oven to 375°F. Mix graham cracker crumbs, butter, and sugar together. Pat into bottom of a 9 x 13 pan and bake for 10 minutes. Cool completely. Mix gelatin with boiling water until dissolved. Set aside and let cool. Beat whipping cream until soft peaks form; add powdered sugar and beat until stiff peaks form, then transfer to a small bowl. Beat cream cheese with sugar. Blend together cooled lemon gelatin, cream cheese mixture, and whipped cream mixture until completely combined. Pour over crust and chill for 2 hours. Just before serving, mix cherry pie filling and mixed berries and spread over top of chilled dessert. Serves 12–15.

&❧ **And Another Thing . . . And Another Thing . . .** You can use whatever fruit you would like to. For my mixed berries I like to use blackberries, raspberries, and blueberries. Also, blueberry pie filling is a nice variation.

Strawberry Shortcake

This is a dish my mother often made for our dinner in the summertime, especially when fresh strawberries were in season. We always had it on strawberry day. Strawberry days were the days that we would get 75–100 quarts of fresh-picked berries from our Amish neighbors for $1.00 a quart. Grandma and my aunts would come over and we would put berries away for winter days. Because farmers always need something substantial to go with this delicious dish, she would usually grill chicken breasts she had marinated for days in Italian dressing or hot dogs the local butcher had made from one of our cows. These hot dogs are nothing like the ones you buy in the store. Dinners like this spell SUMMER to me. I get so nostalgic when I think about those days that it makes me stop and ask myself what I am doing to create these days for my boys. In what ways are you creating these warm, sunny, yummy memories for the ones you love to hold close?

1½ cups	raw or white sugar
½ cup	salted butter, softened
2	eggs
1 tsp.	vanilla extract
2½ tsp.	baking powder
1 tsp.	salt
2¾ cups	flour, divided
1 cup	milk, divided
1 qt.	fresh strawberries, hulled and smashed (add sugar if you like)

Preheat oven to 350°F. Mix sugar, butter, eggs, and vanilla until creamy. Add baking powder, salt, and half the flour. Add ½ cup milk. Mix just until all ingredients are moistened. Add remaining flour and milk. Do not overmix. Pour into a 9 inch baking dish. Bake for 35–40 minutes or until toothpick inserted in center comes out clean. If you want to double the recipe, bake in a 9 x 13 pan and increase baking time a bit. Serve warm with strawberries and milk or ice cream. Most of all, *enjoy*!

Layered Fruit Pizza

Isn't it amazing how certain times of the year just make us want to cook certain foods? Well, this is one of those recipes that screams "Summer!" It is so pretty and colorful.

Sponge cake:

2	eggs
½ cup	hot water
½ cup	raw or white sugar
1 cup	flour
1 tsp.	baking powder
⅛ tsp.	salt
½ tsp.	vanilla extract

Cream cheese mixture:

1½ cups	whipping cream
½ cup	powdered sugar
1 tsp.	vanilla extract
8 oz.	cream cheese

Fresh fruit:

1 cup	pineapple, diced
2 cups	strawberries, sliced
1 cup	blueberries (or frozen blackberries)
2	kiwis, diced
1 (11 oz.) can	mandarin oranges, liquid reserved
1–2 cups	grapes (halved if desired)

Glaze:

1 Tbsp.	Clear Jel or cornstarch
1 cup	water (or mandarin orange liquid)
2 Tbsp.	sugar
1 (3 oz.) box	peach gelatin

Preheat oven to 350°F. For cake, in a medium bowl, beat eggs for 1 minute, then add hot water and sugar and blend until combined. Add flour, baking powder, salt, and vanilla. Pour into a greased 9 x 13 pan (mixture will be runny). Bake for 15–20 minutes.

For cream cheese mixture, beat whipping cream until soft peaks form; add powdered sugar and vanilla, then transfer to a small bowl. Beat cream cheese until smooth. Fold in whipping cream mixture, mixing just until combined. Spread over cooled sponge cake. Layer fruit over cream cheese mixture. I like to randomly place the fruit on top; it gives a nice amount of fruit per each bite. But if you arrange the fruit more neatly, it doesn't take as much to cover the crust.

For glaze, in a small saucepan mix Clear Jel, water, and sugar. Stir together until dissolved. Boil until mixture has thickened, approximately 1–2 minutes. Remove from heat and add peach gelatin. Stir until completely dissolved. When slightly cool, drizzle glaze over fruit pizza. Serves 12–15.

&❧ **And Another Thing . . . And Another Thing . . .** For a Fourth of July dessert, I use this basic recipe and replace the fruit mix with strawberries, blueberries, and blackberries. You can also buy a tube of croissants; roll them out and cut out stars with a cookie cutter. Bake as package specifies. After you have assembled your fruit pizza, randomly place stars on top. It's a fun, creative way to celebrate the holiday!

Grilled Pineapple with Ice Cream

This is such a simple but tasty dessert. Grilling pineapple brings out its natural sweetness.

1	fresh pineapple
½ cup	whipping cream
2 Tbsp.	powdered sugar
1 qt.	vanilla ice cream (or coconut sorbet)
½ cup	caramel ice cream topping
	toasted coconut (optional)
	fresh mint leaves (optional)

Peel pineapple and slice into half-inch-thick rounds. Whip cream until soft peaks form, then add powdered sugar and beat until powdered sugar is incorporated (do not overbeat). Grill pineapple over medium heat for 3 minutes per side. Place 1 piece of grilled pineapple on each plate. Top with 2 small scoops of ice cream, then drizzle with caramel sauce and add a dollop of whipped cream. Garnish each plate with toasted coconut and a fresh mint leaf, if desired. Serves 7–8.

And Another Thing . . . And Another Thing . . . How many times have you been in the produce section of a grocery store attempting to pick out the perfect pineapple? Here are a few tips you might find helpful. If you are looking for a pineapple to serve in the next day or two, turn it over. If there is a little mold growing on the bottom, that's a promising sign it will be sweet. If you are still unsure, pull on a leaf. If it pulls out easy, the pineapple is ripe. If it pulls hard, put it back. If there appear to be no super-ripe pineapples, purchase a less-ripe one but immediately place it in a brown paper bag with a banana, which will aid in the ripening process. If pineapples are on sale, I like to buy one that is ready to eat and one that is green. One final note on pineapples: you will notice that a good pineapple is usually extra sweet at its base. The night before you cut the pineapple, turn it upside down so that its sweet juice can redistribute through the whole pineapple.

Strawberry Pretzel Dessert

This is a wonderful way to use up stale pretzels. I don't know if that's why my family ate this so often, but I really enjoy this tasty, simple dessert.

1 (6 oz.) box	strawberry gelatin
½ cup	boiling water
2 cups	frozen strawberries, thawed and chopped
½ cup	reserved liquid from strawberries
2 cups	pretzels, crushed
½ cup	salted butter, melted
3 Tbsp.	brown sugar
2 cups	whipping cream
½ cup	powdered sugar
16 oz.	cream cheese, softened
½ cup	raw or white sugar
1 tsp.	vanilla extract

In a small bowl dissolve gelatin in boiling water; add strawberries and reserved liquid. Set aside for 45–60 minutes or until gelatin is starting to set up. Preheat oven to 375°F. Mix pretzels, butter, and brown sugar together. Press into bottom of a 9 x 13 pan and bake for 8–10 minutes. Cool completely. Beat whipping cream until soft peaks form; add powdered sugar and set aside. In a large bowl beat cream cheese, sugar, and vanilla until smooth; add whipped cream and mix well. Pour over cooled pretzel crust. Pour cooled gelatin over cream mixture. Allow dessert to set in refrigerator at least 2 hours before serving. Serves 12–14.

Pumpkin Caramel Cheesecake

1½ cups	gingersnaps, crushed (or graham crackers)
1 cup	brown sugar, divided
6 Tbsp.	salted butter, melted
24 oz.	cream cheese, softened
¾ cup	raw or white sugar
1 (15 oz.) can	pumpkin
¼ cup	whipping cream
2 Tbsp.	flour
1 tsp.	vanilla extract
1½ tsp.	cinnamon
½ tsp.	ground cloves
5	eggs, beaten lightly

Streusel topping:

6 Tbsp.	salted butter, melted
1 cup	brown sugar, packed
1 cup	walnuts, chopped
¼ cup	caramel topping

Preheat oven to 350°F. In a small bowl, combine gingersnap crumbs and ¼ cup brown sugar; stir in melted butter. Press into bottom and up sides of greased springform pan and place pan on a cookie sheet. Bake for 8–10 minutes.

Reduce oven temperature to 325°F. In a large bowl, beat cream cheese, sugar, and remaining brown sugar until smooth. Add pumpkin, whipping cream, flour, vanilla, cinnamon, and cloves until blended. Add eggs; beat on low speed just until completely combined. Pour into crust and bake for 1 hour. Add streusel topping and bake an additional 30 minutes.

For streusel topping, combine butter, brown sugar, and walnuts to form a crumbly mixture. Pour gently over hot cheesecake and continue baking as directed. Turn off oven. Cool cheesecake 1 hour in open oven before removing sides of pan. Carefully run a knife around the edge of pan to loosen. Before serving, drizzle caramel topping over top. Serves 14–16.

Coconut Cream Cheesecake

This is a great dessert to serve at your Easter feast.

1¼ cups	graham crackers, crushed
½ cup	flaked coconut
¼ cup	brown sugar
⅓ cup	salted butter, melted
32 oz.	cream cheese, softened
1 cup	raw or white sugar
2 Tbsp.	flour
¾ cup	cream of coconut milk
2 Tbsp.	coconut flavoring
4	eggs, room temperature

Preheat oven to 375°F. For crust, mix together graham crackers, coconut, brown sugar, and butter, and press into bottom of a 9- or 10-inch springform pan. Place springform pan on baking sheet and bake for 8–10 minutes.

Reduce oven to 325°F. Beat cream cheese and sugar until smooth; add flour, coconut milk, and coconut flavoring. Beat in eggs one at a time just until blended. Pour mixture into prepared crust. Bake for 55–65 minutes or until center is almost set. Turn off oven, open oven door, and allow to cool for 1 hour in oven before removing. Refrigerate for 12 hours before serving. Garnish with toasted coconut. Serves 14–16.

Date Nut Pudding with Caramel Sauce

This is one of those recipes that I would never in my life have tried if I were just scrolling through a cookbook. However, it is one of the best family recipes I possess. I made it for my neighbors over the holidays and they raved for days. The assembly of this cake is odd, but it works!

We have this dessert at every Thanksgiving and Christmas dinner with my extended family. When my mother came from Ohio to assist us after the birth of my second son, this was one of the desserts my husband wanted her to make. He did not grow up with this dish but has come to love it as much as my aunts, uncles, and cousins do.

1 cup	chopped dates (or chopped dates with oat flour)
1 cup	boiling water
1 Tbsp.	salted butter
1 cup	flour
1 cup	raw or white sugar
1 tsp.	baking powder
2	eggs, beaten
1 tsp.	vanilla extract
¼ tsp.	salt
¼ tsp.	cinnamon
½ cup	walnuts, chopped (optional)

Caramel sauce:

2 cups	brown sugar
3½ cups	water, divided
¼ cup	salted butter
½ cup	Clear Jel (or cornstarch)
2 tsp.	maple flavoring or vanilla extract

Whipped cream:

2 cups	whipping cream
⅓ cup	powdered sugar
¼ tsp.	cinnamon

Garnish:

2	bananas, peeled and sliced (optional)

Preheat oven to 350°F. In a small bowl, combine dates with boiling water and butter. Allow to set for 10 minutes. Pour mixture into a greased 9 x 9 pan. In a small bowl, mix by hand flour, sugar, baking powder, eggs, vanilla, salt, cinnamon, and walnuts. Spread over date mixture. Bake for 25–30 minutes. Cool completely and cut into small squares.

For caramel sauce, mix brown sugar, 2½ cups water, and butter in a saucepan and boil for 20 minutes to reduce liquid. Stir frequently. Mix remaining 1 cup water with Clear Jel until dissolved completely, then add to boiling liquid. Cook until mixture thickens, approximately 2–3 minutes. Remove from heat and add flavoring. Cool completely in the refrigerator.

Beat whipping cream until soft peaks form, then add powdered sugar and cinnamon and beat until stiff peaks form.

To assemble, take a glass trifle bowl (this dessert is very attractive because it's layered) and layer half of cake, half of sauce, half of whipped cream, and banana slices, if desired. Repeat. Serves 14–16.

And Another Thing . . . And Another Thing . . . In an effort to manage my time efficiently, I like to make the caramel sauce while the dates are setting and cooling in the pan. If you have leftovers, this dish only continues to develop over time. The bananas do not hold up very well, so you may want to take them off, but the rest of it is delish!

Graham Cracker Pudding

I remember my mother making this dish every time she wanted to do something special for my father. It was often his birthday dessert. My father will eat just about anything (except mushrooms); he is the easiest person to cook for. I know sometimes he ate food that had things growing on it simply because he would come in from the field and want some quick lunch! To this day his favorite meal is a simple offering of mom's homemade meatloaf, scalloped potatoes, and graham cracker pudding. I think this probably became a favorite for my mother to whip up because it takes very basic ingredients that come from the farm, things we always had on hand.

3	eggs, separated
½ cup	milk
1 cup	raw or white sugar
1 pkg.	Knox gelatin (1 Tbsp.)
1 cup	graham cracker crumbs
6 Tbsp.	salted butter, melted
1½ cups	whipping cream
¼ cup	powdered sugar
1 tsp.	vanilla extract

In a small saucepan, stir egg yolks well and add milk and sugar. Cook over medium-high heat and bring to a boil; allow to boil for 1 minute. Add gelatin. Cool mixture in refrigerator for 35–45 minutes. While egg yolk mixture is chilling, crush graham crackers and add melted butter; stir together well and set aside. Beat egg whites until stiff peaks form, and add to cooled egg yolk mixture. Beat whipping cream until soft peaks form; sweeten with powdered sugar and vanilla. Stir into egg mixture. Press graham cracker crumbs onto bottom and sides of serving bowl, reserving ½ cup of the crumbs. Place pudding mixture into bowl and sprinkle with remaining cracker crumbs. Refrigerate for 2–3 hours or until set. Serves 4–6.

Pumpkin Pie Squares

¾ cup	salted butter, softened
1⅓ cups	all-purpose flour
¾ cup	brown sugar, packed
1 cup	oatmeal
½ cup	pecans, chopped
8 oz.	cream cheese, softened
½ cup	raw or white sugar
3	eggs
1 (15 oz.) can	pumpkin
1 Tbsp.	cinnamon
⅛ tsp.	nutmeg
⅛ tsp.	ground ginger

Preheat oven to 350°F. Mix butter, flour, and brown sugar together. Mixture will be crumbly. Stir in oatmeal and pecans. Reserve 1 cup of crumb topping; press remaining mixture into bottom of a greased 9 x 13 baking pan. Bake for 15 minutes. Beat cream cheese and sugar until smooth. Add eggs, pumpkin, and spices; mix until smooth and well blended. Pour over crust; sprinkle with reserved crumbs and additional cinnamon. Bake for 25–30 minutes, or until set. Serves 14–16.

Mom's Homemade Ice Cream

This has to be the best homemade ice cream ever. Sometimes homemade ice cream can be icy, but we had this yummy, creamy stuff when we celebrated my uncles' and aunts' birthdays, when it was fresh strawberry season or red raspberry season, or even when it was snowing outside. My mother often would use snow instead of ice in her ice cream maker.

Last summer, when my grandfather was diagnosed with cancer, my mother made this rich, delicious treat for him three times in the three short weeks he was home from the hospital. He requested it for Father's Day and ate it many times thereafter for breakfast. It was her way of showering him with all the love she could give. And it reminded the rest of the family of days gone by when we would get together to celebrate birthdays and special events and eat as much of that creamy goodness as we wanted.

6	eggs
1 cup	raw or white sugar
1 cup	brown sugar
1 (5.1 oz.) box	instant vanilla pudding mix
1 Tbsp.	vanilla extract
2 cups	half-and-half
4 cups	milk

Beat eggs for 6 minutes until they are light and fluffy (this is key to good ice cream). Add sugars. Beat well. Add vanilla pudding, vanilla extract, and half-and-half. Pour into a 6-quart ice cream maker. Add milk. Place ice and salt around ice cream maker per manufacturer's instructions. Start and follow instructions until finished. Serves 6–8.

• **And Another Thing . . . And Another Thing . . .** I am aware that there are raw eggs in this recipe. All I can say in its defense is my family has eaten this for years, and we are healthy and strong and have never gotten sick from them.

Mocha Latte Ice Cream

If you love chocolate and coffee, this will be like a party in your mouth.

6	eggs
1 cup	raw or white sugar
1 cup	brown sugar
⅓ cup	instant coffee
¼ cup	warm water
1 (5.1 oz.) pkg.	instant chocolate pudding
½ tsp.	salt
½ cup	half-and-half
4 cups	milk
1 cup	pecans, chopped and toasted (optional)

Beat eggs for 6 minutes until they are light and fluffy (this is key to good ice cream). Add sugars. Beat well. Dissolve coffee granules in warm water. Add coffee, pudding, salt, and half-and-half to egg mixture, and mix well. Pour into a 6-quart ice cream maker. Fill with 4 cups milk and pecans. Place ice and salt around ice cream maker per manufacturer's instructions. Start and follow instructions until finished. Serves 6–8.

🐝 **And Another Thing . . . And Another Thing . . .** The key to successful homemade ice cream is following the ice cream maker's salt instructions to a tee.

Quick Pumpkin Ice Cream

1.5 qts.	vanilla ice cream, softened
1 cup	canned pumpkin
½ cup	brown sugar
1 tsp.	cinnamon

Garnish:

gingersnap cookies

whipped cream

cinnamon

Place the first four ingredients in a bowl and beat well. Pour into an 8 x 8 pan. Cover; freeze for 3–4 hours. Let soften slightly before scooping. Serve in small bowls; garnish with gingersnaps, whipped cream, and cinnamon, if desired. Serves 6–8.

Food for Thought

We were both eight, my aunt Rose and I. As was our summer tradition, my grandfather, a cabinet installer, allowed us both to accompany him to work in his big box truck. This day turned out to be great because there were multiple houses at the job site, not just a single house with piles of dirt. We didn't know what a subdivision was—we just knew we liked this job site, which had a house with a concrete-floored garage. We rode our bikes around and around that little garage. We were two little girls with no care in the world other than living life as we knew it, until all of a sudden Rose said, "There's a man coming after us with a big stick!" I just kept cruising, because we weren't doing anything wrong, until suddenly he was there—and oh, my goodness. This wasn't just any stick—this was a BIG stick.

I still feel my heart race today as I recall that moment. I don't know if I have *ever* been so scared in my life. We raced as fast as our little legs could take us to where Grandpa was. Grandpa tells the story that all he heard was frantic, "Grandpa/Daddy! Grandpa/Daddy!" We dropped our bikes and hurried toward him and safety. We were so shook up we couldn't even breathe. I will never forget my grandpa's words to that man. "Those are my girls," he said. The man immediately left, muttering "Sorry" under his breath.

I hadn't thought about this story in years, but last summer as I was racing the clock to see my grandpa one last time, there it was in my mind. I relived the words, "Those are my girls," and the Lord used it to say to me, *Dawn, you are my girl*. That's all I needed for that moment. I had heard Jesus in those early morning hours as I was beginning the grieving process. I knew when I left Grandpa at the end of that week I would not see him again on earth, but I was deeply loved by my grandpa and by Jesus—I am his girl!

8

Cookies, Cakes, and Bars

Thanksgiving 2005 was our second Thanksgiving as a new start-up business at The Farmer's Wife market. Pies and dinner roll orders were arriving in droves. We were trying to anticipate demand, fill orders, and make as many pies as possible. We had an order from one customer for twelve pumpkin pies. We did our normal prep: we rolled out the pie shells, whipped up the pumpkin filling made with real cream, and placed them in the oven to bake. When they came out of the convection oven they looked beautiful. There was no clue something might be wrong with them. For some reason we tasted an extra one (we RARELY did this) and clearly there was a problem. We had forgotten to put sugar in the pumpkin mixture!

There was no salvaging any part of those pies, not even the crust. For a new business owner who still didn't know whether her business was going to succeed or fail, twelve pies was a big deal. I think I cried that day when I threw those pies into the dumpster. We ended up making twenty-four pies to fill the original order. I share this story to say that sometimes—a lot of times—there are anxieties in our life that are really quite small but feel big, and we exhaust a lot of emotional energy wondering if the "situation" will be to our ruin. We pray, we wrestle, we worry, we struggle, and we don't even realize that God in his almighty faithfulness is doing something so much bigger in our lives than seeing to our comfort. He is inviting us to trust him, to cling to him in

When baking, always adjust your baking time to your oven's settings. I found while working on this project that all ovens bake differently. When in doubt, underbake an item. You can always add a few more minutes, but if you overbake it, it's impossible to undo.

our anxiety, to rest and to see him in the little and big details of our lives. He invites us to fall into his arms, trusting that where he leads us we will faithfully follow. When we understand and grasp that life really isn't about comfort but about being "conformed into his image" (see Rom. 8:29), we can embrace the little and big things, and in those hard times know that we are experiencing growth.

Peanut Butter Whoopie Pies

Oh, my goodness. If you like peanut butter and chocolate, I promise you will have a very hard time eating just one of these!

2 cups	miniature semisweet chocolate chips
2 Tbsp.	milk
¾ cup	salted butter, softened
¼ cup	creamy peanut butter
2	eggs
½ cup	milk
1½ cups	raw or white sugar
1 tsp.	baking soda
1 tsp.	baking powder
½ tsp.	salt
1 tsp.	vanilla extract
½ cup	unsweetened cocoa powder
2¾ cups	white wheat flour (or 3 cups all-purpose flour)

Filling:

¾ cup	salted butter, softened
¾ cup	creamy peanut butter
¾ cup	marshmallow cream
1¾ cups	powdered sugar

Preheat oven to 350°F. In a small saucepan over very low heat, combine chocolate chips and 2 tablespoons milk, stirring constantly until melted. Set aside.

Beat butter and peanut butter until well mixed. Add eggs and beat. Add milk, sugar, baking soda, baking powder, salt, and vanilla; beat until mixed. Add cocoa powder and flour and stir until combined. Stir in melted chocolate. Drop by teaspoons onto ungreased cookie sheets. Optional: sprinkle with extra chocolate or peanut butter chips. Bake for 11–13 minutes. Cool completely.

For filling, mix all 4 ingredients together. If you need to get a smoother consistency, just add a little milk. Leftover filling will keep well in the refrigerator for 4 weeks, or can be frozen. To assemble, spread bottom side of cookie with 1–2 tablespoons filling and top with another cookie to form a sandwich. You can individually wrap with plastic wrap or place in a container. They freeze well! Yields 2 dozen.

And Another Thing . . . And Another Thing . . . I always use raw sugar and white wheat flour in this recipe to make them a little healthier, and you would never know.

Butterscotch Cookies

I do love all things rich and buttery. These are no exception.

1 cup	half-and-half
1 Tbsp.	vinegar
½ cup	salted butter, softened
1½ cups	brown sugar, packed
2	eggs
1 tsp.	vanilla extract
1 tsp.	baking soda
½ tsp.	baking powder
½ tsp.	salt
2¾ cups	all-purpose flour (or 2½ cups white wheat flour)

Preheat oven to 350°F. Combine half-and-half and vinegar. Set aside. Beat butter and brown sugar until well blended. Add eggs and vanilla and beat until fluffy, approximately 2 minutes. Add baking soda, baking powder, and salt. Beat well. Add flour alternately with the half-and-half mixture, beginning and ending with flour. Drop by spoonfuls onto a greased cookie sheet and bake for 12–14 minutes. I tend to underbake these; if you want to be sure these cookies are done, insert toothpick in the center of a cookie, and if it comes out clean, then you know they are ready. Frost with Browned Butter Frosting or Brown Sugar Frosting (below). Yields 3 dozen.

Browned Butter Frosting

½ cup	salted butter, softened
3½ cups	powdered sugar
4 Tbsp.	milk, divided
pinch	salt
½ tsp.	vanilla extract
	walnuts, chopped (optional)

In a small saucepan, brown butter on stovetop (about 4–5 minutes) over high heat. Remove from heat and add powdered sugar, 2 tablespoons milk, salt, and vanilla. Beat to combine, and add more milk to reach desired consistency. Beat until smooth. Frost cookies and sprinkle with chopped walnuts, if desired.

Brown Sugar Frosting

½ cup	salted butter
1 cup	brown sugar
¼ cup	milk
⅛ tsp.	salt
1 tsp.	vanilla extract
2½–3 cups	powdered sugar

Melt butter in a small saucepan over medium heat. Add brown sugar and cook for 2 minutes, stirring constantly. Remove from heat and add milk, salt, and vanilla. Gradually add powdered sugar until desired consistency. Beat until sugar is completely mixed in; frost cookies while frosting is still warm. If frosting becomes too stiff, add a little hot water to thin it.

🍃 **And Another Thing . . . And Another Thing . . .** In these cookies, you can substitute the half-and-half and vinegar with 1 cup buttermilk.

Pumpkin Maple Whoopie Pies

These cookies have a wonderfully divine autumn note to them.

2 cups	brown sugar, lightly packed
1 cup	canola oil
3 cups	pumpkin purée
2	eggs
2 tsp.	vanilla extract
1 Tbsp.	cinnamon
1 tsp.	ground ginger
½ tsp.	ground cloves
3 cups	all-purpose flour
1 tsp.	baking powder
1 tsp.	baking soda
1 tsp.	salt

Filling:

8 oz.	cream cheese, softened
3 cups	powdered sugar
1½ tsp.	maple extract

Preheat oven to 350°F. Beat together brown sugar, oil, pumpkin, eggs, and vanilla. Add cinnamon, ginger, cloves, flour, baking powder, baking soda, and salt. Mix just until well blended. With an ice cream scoop, drop onto a greased cookie sheet. Bake for 12–14 minutes, or until toothpick inserted in center comes out clean. Remove from oven and let cookies cool completely on rack. The cookies should be firm when touched.

For filling, beat cream cheese until smooth. Add powdered sugar and maple extract and beat until smooth. If mixture seems a bit too thin, refrigerate for 30 minutes before filling cookies. To fill cookies, take one cookie and spread 1–2 tablespoons of filling on the bottom; add another cookie on top to form a sandwich. Yields 2 dozen.

Double Chocolate Chip Cookies

1 cup	salted butter, softened
¾ cup	brown sugar, packed
2	eggs
1 tsp.	vanilla extract
1 (3.9 oz.) pkg.	instant chocolate pudding mix
2½ cups	flour
1 tsp.	baking soda
1 cup	semisweet chocolate chips

Preheat oven to 350°F. Cream butter and sugar. Add eggs, vanilla, and chocolate pudding mix. Beat until smooth and creamy. Add flour and baking soda. Stir until mixed, then add chocolate chips. Batter will be stiff. Drop onto cookie sheet and press down with the back of your spoon. Bake for 10–14 minutes. Do not overbake. These can be a little tricky to bake because the dough is dark. You may want to do a test cookie before you bake all of them. Yields 2 dozen.

🐌 **And Another Thing . . . And Another Thing . . .** For a variation to this cookie you can cut the amount of chocolate chips in half and add half M&Ms. You can also add ½ cup of chopped nuts to this batter. If you want a healthier version, use 2¼ cups white wheat flour instead of 2½ cups all-purpose flour.

Macadamia, White Chocolate, and Cranberry Cookies

½ cup	salted butter, softened
⅔ cup	brown sugar
1	egg
1 Tbsp.	milk
1 tsp.	vanilla extract
1½ cups	flour
1 tsp.	baking soda
½ tsp.	baking powder
½ tsp.	salt
½ cup	white chocolate chips
½ cup	macadamia nuts, coarsely chopped
½ cup	dried cranberries

Preheat oven to 350°F. Cream butter and sugar together. Add egg, milk, and vanilla. Mix well. Add flour, baking soda, baking powder, and salt. Beat just until mixed well. Mix in white chocolate chips, nuts, and cranberries. Drop in 1-inch balls on a greased cookie sheet and bake for 8–10 minutes. Do not overbake. Yields 1½ dozen.

Sour Cream Christmas Cookies

These are my Grandma Tena's specialty. I will never forget a treacherous, snowy drive home after a wonderful December day spent at her house making more cookies than three families would ever need. We frosted, sprinkled, sampled, and then set out for home. Little did we know when we left that our hard work would be damaged. We landed in the ditch due to snow and ice, and the cookie tubs did not stay in their places. However, they still tasted good. This annual tradition has become a precious memory, because five years later my grandma went home to be with Jesus at a very young age. I treasure memories of her kitchen and love to make these every Christmas in celebration of the love she shared with our family and the fond memories I have of being in her home!

What recipes evoke special memories for you? Make them often in celebration of the wonderful time you have spent with the ones you love. The recipe may not only be good to your taste buds, but the memories it evokes may also instantly take you back to those special times. Without even realizing it, you will be reliving the "good old days."

2 cups	raw or white sugar
1 cup	salted butter, softened
1 cup	sour cream
2 tsp.	baking soda
2 Tbsp.	cream or milk
4	egg yolks
6–6½ cups	flour

Preheat oven to 375°F. Beat sugar, butter, and sour cream until well blended. Dissolve baking soda in cream; add to mixture and then add egg yolks. Mix gently. Add most of the flour and stir completely. If the dough is too sticky add enough flour to get a consistency you can roll out. If you add too much flour, you will get a dough that is too stiff. Roll dough to ⅓–½ inch thick, cut into shapes, then transfer to ungreased baking sheet and bake for 8–10 minutes. Do not overbake. Frost with your favorite icing or frosting. Yields 4 dozen.

🐦 **And Another Thing . . . And Another Thing . . .** Refrigerate dough for 60 minutes if you have time; it will make cookies easier to roll out. Also, you can substitute half of the flour with whole wheat flour. Just cut the amount of flour back to 5½ cups total.

Chocolate Meringue Bars

You can please both crowds with this: those who like coconut and those who do not. Follow the instructions and when you get to the nuts and coconut, only sprinkle half of the coconut on one half of the pan.

1 cup	salted butter, softened
½ cup	brown sugar
½ cup	raw or white sugar
2	egg yolks
2¼ cups	all-purpose flour (or 2 cups white wheat flour)
½ tsp.	baking powder
¼ tsp.	salt
1½ cups	semisweet chocolate chips
1 cup	chopped nuts (optional)
1 cup	flaked coconut (optional)

Meringue:

2	egg whites
½ cup	brown sugar
⅛ tsp.	baking powder

Preheat oven to 350°F. Cream butter and sugars. Add egg yolks and beat well. Add flour, baking powder, and salt. Blend until mixed. Mixture will be crumbly. Press into bottom of a 9 x 13 pan with a fork. Sprinkle with chocolate chips, nuts, and coconut, if desired. For meringue, beat egg whites until stiff. Gradually beat in brown sugar and baking powder. Spread over chocolate chips and nuts. Bake for 5 minutes at 350°F, then reduce oven temperature to 300°F and continue to bake for 20–25 minutes, until meringue looks crisp. Allow to set for 1 hour before cutting. Yields 16–18 bars.

> **And Another Thing . . . And Another Thing . . .** If meringue is too moist after cooling, be sure to adjust your baking time the next time you make these. When the meringue is perfect these bars are so delicious!

Chocolate Chip Peanut Butter Oatmeal Bars

If you are looking for a quick dessert, this is the one. You can mix it up in ten minutes; what takes the longest is the baking time. I like good recipes like this that I can create without investing a lot of time in my busy day.

2 cups	oatmeal
1½ cups	flour
1 cup	brown sugar
1 tsp.	baking powder
¾ tsp.	salt
1 cup	salted butter, melted
1 (14 oz.) can	sweetened condensed milk
¾ cup	peanut butter
1½ cups	chocolate chips
1 cup	toasted pecans, chopped (optional)

Preheat oven to 375°F. Mix together oatmeal, flour, brown sugar, baking powder, and salt; add melted butter and mix until crumbly. Reserve 1⅓ cups of the mixture and press remaining crumbs into bottom of a 9 x 13 pan. Bake for 12 minutes and remove from oven; crust will not be completely baked. Combine sweetened condensed milk and peanut butter, and pour over warm crust. Sprinkle chocolate chips on top, then sprinkle with reserved crumbs and toasted pecans, if using. Bake for 20 minutes. Do not overbake. Yields 16–18 bars.

Lime Macaroon Bars

2 cups	flour, divided
2¼ cups	raw or white sugar, divided
½ cup	salted butter, melted
½ cup	pecans, crushed
5	eggs
⅔ cup	lime juice
2 tsp.	lime zest
1 tsp.	baking soda
¼ tsp.	salt
1 cup	flaked coconut
½ cup	powdered sugar

Garnish:

lime or orange zest curls

mint leaves

Preheat oven to 350°F. Mix together 1¾ cups flour, ½ cup sugar, butter, and pecans; mixture will be crumbly. Spread into bottom of a 9 x 13 pan. Bake for 15 minutes or until lightly golden. In a large mixing bowl, beat eggs until light and fluffy, approximately 3–4 minutes (this is key to a nice bar). Add remaining 1¾ cups sugar and lime juice. Mix well. Add lime zest, remaining ¼ cup flour, baking soda, and salt. Pour over prepared crust. Sprinkle coconut on top. Bake for 20–25 minutes. Let cool for 1 hour. Cut into 2-inch squares and sprinkle with powdered sugar. Garnish as desired. Yields 16–18 bars.

And Another Thing . . . And Another Thing . . . This is great to serve at a summer picnic! If some of your family or guests don't like coconut, only add it to half of the pan.

Granola Balls

These are delicious, wholesome, and truly satisfying! I love giving my boys these as a snack. It is so fun for Camden and me to make "golf balls" as he calls them. The best part about these "little balls of sweet" is that there is no sugar in them. Your body is able to digest honey better than sugar, which makes this recipe extra good for you!

1 cup	honey
1 cup	peanut butter
⅛ tsp.	salt
3 cups	oatmeal (quick or old-fashioned)
1 cup	flaked coconut
½ cup	wheat germ or bran
2 Tbsp.	flax seed
1 cup	chocolate chips
½ cup	dried cranberries or pecans, chopped (optional)

Beat together honey, peanut butter, and salt. Add oatmeal, coconut, wheat germ, flax seed, chocolate chips, and cranberries or pecans, if desired. Stir until well mixed. Roll into golf ball–size balls or smaller. Refrigerate if desired. Yields 30 balls. These freeze well.

Strawberry Cheesecake Bars

This is so fun to serve when it is strawberry season. Slice your strawberries all different ways, and place one on each piece. I like to put a whole berry on one piece, and strawberry leaves or a strawberry blossom on another piece. Sliver one berry but don't cut it the whole way through, and put it on another piece. Cut one the opposite way you cut the others. Be sure to keep as many of the green tops on the berries as possible. There is something about looking at food, both its presentation and the creativity behind it. Your eyes can't take it all in—and in that moment you are drawn in. In that moment you see the creativity of God. He writes it in different places and in different ways for each of us.

1½ cups	graham crackers, crushed
6 Tbsp.	salted butter, melted
1 Tbsp.	raw or white sugar
1 (6 oz.) pkg.	strawberry gelatin
¾ cup	boiling water
1 cup	fresh strawberries, crushed (or frozen, thawed)
1½ cups	whipping cream
1 cup	powdered sugar
16 oz.	cream cheese, softened

Preheat oven to 350°F. In a small bowl combine graham crackers, butter, and sugar. Mix well. Press into a 9 x 13 baking dish and bake for 10–12 minutes. Cool.

In a small bowl combine gelatin and water; mix well and immediately add crushed strawberries. Stir until gelatin is dissolved. Refrigerate for 30 minutes. In another bowl beat whipping cream until soft peaks form, then add powdered sugar. Set aside. In a large bowl beat cream cheese until very smooth. Add slightly cooled strawberry mixture to cream cheese; beat well. Fold in whipped cream. Pour over cooled crust. Cover and refrigerate 8–12 hours. Cut into 2-inch squares and garnish with additional strawberries as desired. Yields 16–18 bars.

Scotties

1 cup	brown sugar, packed
½ cup	raw or white sugar
1 cup	salted butter
2 lg.	eggs
2 tsp.	vanilla extract
2 cups	all-purpose flour (or 1¾ cups white wheat flour)
1 Tbsp.	baking powder
½ tsp.	salt
1 cup	white chocolate chips
1 cup	unsalted macadamia nuts, chopped (or walnuts)

Preheat oven to 350°F. Cream sugars and butter together. Add eggs and vanilla, and mix well. Add flour, baking powder, and salt. Stir until mixed; add white chocolate chips and nuts. Pour into an ungreased 9 x 13 pan and bake for 35–40 minutes. Yields 16–18 bars.

ॐ **And Another Thing . . . And Another Thing . . .** If you want to add an extra touch to these bars, cut into 1-inch squares then melt additional white chocolate chips and drizzle across the top of the bars. Or you can turn this into a dessert by simply cutting the bars, topping each with a dot of vanilla ice cream, and drizzling with caramel sauce. Be sure to brew a fresh pot of hot, steamy coffee if you serve it this way. Coffee is the perfect complement to this yummy sweet treat!

Toasted Butter Pecan Cake

Our friend Joel was turning fifty, and my three-year-old Camden overheard a conversation about his birthday and promptly informed me what we should do. He said, "Mom, we need to make him a 'take' and give him a gift. What kind of 'take' you going to make him?" Well, when I told my son I wasn't going to make Joel a cake, he melted me into a puddle. His giving spirit has inspired me multiple times. When we buy special treats at the grocery store he almost always saves some for his daddy, who is at work and can't have part of our treat. I reconsidered my decision about that cake. It was more than just making a cake for our friend—it was about continuing to impart a giving spirit to my son. I want him to understand that we celebrate people in our lives that we love, and that when we "give away" we get so much more in return. There is a deep sense of peace that washes over my soul every time I share with someone! Who in your life right now could you make a "take" for and give a piece of your heart to? Who could you celebrate today? It doesn't have to be something big. My son and I compromised that day, and delivered Joel a cupcake made with love by all of us.

2 cups	pecans, chopped
1 cup	salted butter, softened
2 cups	raw or white sugar
4	eggs
2 tsp.	almond extract
3 cups	all-purpose flour
2 tsp.	baking powder
½ tsp.	salt
1 cup	milk

Frosting:

16 oz.	cream cheese, softened
½ cup	salted butter, softened
5 cups	powdered sugar
2 tsp.	almond extract
1–2 Tbsp.	milk

Preheat oven to 350°F. Place chopped pecans on a cookie sheet and toast for 10–15 minutes. Let cool. In a large mixing bowl, cream butter and sugar. Add eggs one at a time, beating well after each addition. Add almond extract. Add flour, baking powder, salt, and milk; beat just until combined. Fold in 1 cup of toasted pecans. Pour into 3 greased 8-inch round baking pans or 2 greased 9-inch round baking pans. Bake for 22–28 minutes or until toothpick inserted in center comes out clean. Do not overbake. Cool for 10 minutes before removing from pans.

For frosting, in a large mixing bowl beat cream cheese, butter, powdered sugar, and almond extract. Add enough milk to achieve the frosting consistency you like. Frost cake and sprinkle remaining toasted pecans on top. Serves 14–16.

🍂 **And Another Thing . . . And Another Thing . . .** To make this dish really sing, add a fresh mint sprig and a raspberry to each plate when you serve it.

Texas Sheet Cake

This is a very simple cake to make. It's hard for me to put a box cake mix into my grocery cart because of all the ingredients I cannot pronounce listed on the side (not that I don't ever do it). Cake mixes are simple and convenient, but when I realized that making this cake only required one messy dish, I was hooked.

1 cup	salted butter
1 cup	water
¼ cup	cocoa powder
½ cup	buttermilk (or sour cream)
¼ tsp.	salt
1 tsp.	vanilla extract
2 cups	raw or white sugar
2	eggs, beaten
1 tsp.	baking soda
2 cups	flour (1¾ cups if using wheat flour)

Frosting:

½ cup	salted butter
6 Tbsp.	milk (or half-and-half)
¼ cup	cocoa powder
1 tsp.	vanilla extract
3¾ cups	powdered sugar
1 cup	nuts (optional)

Preheat oven to 350°F. In a small saucepan combine butter, water, and cocoa powder; bring to a boil, stirring frequently. Remove from heat and add buttermilk, salt, vanilla, sugar, eggs, baking soda, and flour. Pour into a greased jelly roll pan and bake for 25 minutes. You can also bake this in a prepared 9 x 13 pan or Bundt pan (I like to grease the Bundt pan and then dust it with cocoa powder instead of flour, so that the cake pops out of the pan easier and doesn't have white flour showing). For a Bundt pan, you need to adjust the baking time by adding 8–10 more minutes.

For frosting, in a small saucepan melt butter, milk, and cocoa powder and cook just until boiling. Remove from heat and add vanilla and powdered sugar.

Beat with a small hand mixer until light and fluffy. Stir in nuts, if desired, and spread onto warm cake. Serves 24.

🐦 **And Another Thing . . . And Another Thing . . .** You can also frost this cake with Mocha Buttercream Frosting (page 205) and garnish with a chocolate bar grated with a vegetable peeler, or Brown Sugar Frosting II (page 203). To make a very simple but elegant dessert, bake this in a Bundt pan, cut into 3 pieces horizontally and layer with raspberry cream (beat 2 cups whipping cream, ¼ cup powdered sugar, and 1 cup frozen red raspberries, thawed and drained). Drizzle with above frosting. Also, if you bake this cake in a Bundt pan you will need only a half batch of frosting.

Pumpkin Bars with Cinnamon Cream Cheese Icing

This is such a fun and simple dessert to serve in the fall. For a unique touch, cut into diamond shapes, place a pecan half in the middle, or sprinkle with cinnamon.

4	eggs
1 cup	canola oil
2 cups	raw or white sugar
1 (15 oz.) can	pumpkin
½ tsp.	salt
2 tsp.	cinnamon
1 tsp.	baking soda
1 tsp.	baking powder
1¾ cups	white wheat flour (or 2 cups all-purpose flour)
1 cup	walnuts or pecans, chopped

Frosting:

8 oz.	cream cheese, softened
5 Tbsp.	salted butter, softened
2½ cups	powdered sugar
1 Tbsp.	milk
1 tsp.	cinnamon
1 tsp.	vanilla extract

Preheat oven to 350°F. Beat eggs very well (this is key). Add oil, sugar, and pumpkin; mix well. Add salt, cinnamon, baking soda, baking powder, and flour. Stir until mixed completely. Add nuts. Pour into an ungreased jelly roll pan. Bake for 20 minutes or until toothpick inserted in center comes out clean.

For frosting, beat cream cheese and butter until smooth. Add powdered sugar, milk, cinnamon, and vanilla. Beat until smooth. You may need to add more milk to reach desired consistency. Frost bars after they have completely cooled. Yields 24 bars.

Brown Sugar Frosting II

I really like this recipe because it doesn't seem to mess up every bowl in my kitchen. My dear grandmother used to make this as a drizzle for angel food cake. I remember many Sunday lunches at her house with an angel food cake frosted with this frosting. One lick of this frosting still takes me back to her yellow-countered kitchen. This frosting is also great on yellow cakes and cinnamon rolls.

½ cup	salted butter
1 cup	brown sugar
2½–3 cups	powdered sugar
⅛ tsp.	salt
1 tsp.	vanilla extract
¼ cup	milk

Melt butter in a small saucepan over medium-high heat. Add brown sugar and cook for 1–2 minutes, stirring constantly. Remove from heat and add powdered sugar, salt, and vanilla. Gradually add milk. Warning: the caramel mixture gets stiff quickly and tends to be lumpy if you don't beat it with an electric hand mixer. While still warm, pour over your baked good. If icing becomes too stiff, add a little hot water to thin it. Yields 2½ cups.

Cream Cheese Frosting

8 oz.	cream cheese, softened
¼ cup	salted butter, softened
1 Tbsp.	milk
1 tsp.	vanilla extract
⅛ tsp.	salt
4 cups	powdered sugar

Beat cream cheese, butter, milk, vanilla, and salt in a large bowl until fluffy. Gradually add powdered sugar until smooth. If you would like it to be a little thinner, add a bit more milk. If you want it stiffer, add more powdered sugar. Yields 3 cups.

Buttercream Frosting

⅓ cup   salted butter, softened
3½ cups   powdered sugar
6 Tbsp.   milk
1 tsp.   vanilla extract
pinch   salt

Cream butter until fluffy. Add powdered sugar, milk, vanilla, and salt. Beat until smooth, light, and fluffy. If you would like it thicker, add more powdered sugar; if you would like it thinner, add more milk. Yields 2 cups.

Chocolate Buttercream Frosting

⅓ cup   salted butter, softened
3½ cups   powdered sugar
6 Tbsp.   milk
2 Tbsp.   cocoa powder
pinch   salt

Cream butter until fluffy. Add powdered sugar, milk, cocoa powder, and salt. Beat until smooth, light, and fluffy. If you would like it thicker, add more powdered sugar; if you would like it thinner, add more milk. Yields 2 cups.

Mocha Buttercream Frosting

⅓ cup salted butter, softened
3½ cups powdered sugar
5 Tbsp. milk
pinch salt
1 Tbsp. instant coffee granules
1 Tbsp. hot water

Cream butter until fluffy. Add powdered sugar, milk, and salt. Dissolve coffee in hot water; add to mixture. Beat until smooth, light, and fluffy. If you would like it thicker, add more powdered sugar; if you would like it thinner, add more milk. Yields 2 cups.

Food for Thought

While food and drink nourish our physical body, God's Word and a personal relationship with Jesus nourish our soul. If you have never felt the deeply freeing experience of knowing your sins are forgiven and knowing you stand clean before Jesus, today could be your day of salvation. I invite you to pray something like:

Father, I know that I have broken your laws and my sins have separated me from you. I am truly sorry, and I want to turn away from my past sinful life and turn toward you. Please forgive me, and help me avoid sinning again. I believe that your son Jesus Christ died for my sins, was resurrected from the dead, is alive, and hears my prayer. I invite Jesus to become Lord of my life, to rule and reign in my heart from this day forward. Please send your Holy Spirit to help me obey you and do your will for the rest of my life. In Jesus's name I pray, amen.

I would also encourage you to find a godly person to walk alongside and mentor you.

9

Simple Do-It-Yourself Recipes

Something I absolutely love about Mennonite culture is that we are taught to be very innovative and frugal, sometimes almost to a fault. (It is a good thing to be frugal, but sometimes frugal crosses the line into stingy and I am not an advocate of stingy!) We do know how to take things and redeem what could be lost. Below are some recipes to make your dollar stretch when it comes to cleaning products, and some recipes that will allow you to feel the satisfaction of making something a little healthier to serve your family. Pick and choose what works for you—some will and some won't. There is a lot of hype to simplify and make *everything* at home. But free yourself from that pressure, and begin to take positive steps toward saving money and having healthier products in your home—gradually. Real, positive changes in our lives come one tiny baby step at a time. With time, it will be easier to make more changes to homemade products.

Christmas Potpourri

One early December day, I needed a wonderful, homey scent wafting through my home to help celebrate the season. This was just the ticket.

1	orange, halved
1 tsp.	whole cloves
1 tsp.	whole allspice
2	cinnamon sticks
2	bay leaves
4 cups	water

Combine all ingredients and simmer on your stovetop on very low heat for 2–4 hours. You can reuse this mixture the next day as well. Just be sure to add more water as needed.

Taco Seasoning

7 Tbsp.	chili powder
5 Tbsp.	onion salt
3 Tbsp.	garlic powder
5 Tbsp.	cumin
3 Tbsp.	paprika
2 Tbsp.	sugar
	cayenne pepper (to taste)

Mix together all ingredients. Yields 2 cups.

For tacos, use 1–1½ tablespoons of seasoning along with 2 tablespoons of water to season 1 pound of ground beef, chicken, or turkey. Adjust seasoning according to preference.

And Another Thing . . . And Another Thing . . . This is a super easy recipe for taco seasoning. It does not have any MSG in it. Store it in a small container in your spice cabinet. Over the course of time you will save money by not buying taco seasoning packets.

Herbal Butter

2 tsp. each	fresh chives, basil, parsley, and dill (or 1 tsp. each dried)
1 tsp.	garlic powder
1 tsp.	lemon juice
1 cup	salted butter, softened

Mix together and store in refrigerator. It will keep for 3–4 weeks.

🕊 **And Another Thing . . . And Another Thing . . .** This butter is wonderful over fish. You can serve it with bread; it's a great savory approach to dinner. Use it to fry eggs in the morning for breakfast, or melt it over chicken that is almost finished on the grill.

Sundried Tomatoes

This is a great use for all the extra tomatoes from your garden. Plum or roma tomatoes work best for this.

Slice tomatoes paper thin and remove some of the seeds. Lay individually on a cookie sheet lined with parchment paper. Sprinkle lightly with coarse salt or sea salt. Place cookie sheet in a warm oven set at 150–175°F and let the tomatoes dry until shriveled, about 6–8 hours. They should feel dry but still be pliable. Oven-dried tomatoes will not be as dry as commercially dried ones. Store oven-dried tomatoes in an airtight container in the refrigerator for up to 6 months, or in the freezer for 1 year.

🕊 **And Another Thing . . . And Another Thing . . .** These have a wonderfully intense tomato flavor. They will be a bit chewy. They are a great addition to sandwiches, cream cheese, scrambled eggs, soups, pizza, and pasta.

Cream of Celery, Chicken, or Mushroom Soup

There are several reasons you may want to consider making your own condensed soup: you may have slightly aging mushrooms or celery that you need to use up, you started dinner only to discover you don't have a can on hand, you keep hearing about the MSG most canned versions have—or you simply want to make it for pennies instead of spending dollars. There are a few favorite recipes that I am not ready to abandon because of that nasty MSG in the canned versions, so here is a simple recipe you can make in your own kitchen and have on hand.

2 cups	powdered milk
3 Tbsp.	reduced sodium chicken bouillon
3 Tbsp.	onion flakes
2 tsp.	dried basil
2 tsp.	dried parsley
1 tsp.	garlic powder
⅛ tsp.	black pepper
½ tsp.	dried thyme
1½ cups	cornstarch
2 Tbsp.	diced celery (or ½ cup freeze-dried mushrooms or chopped cooked chicken)

Mix together all ingredients except celery, mushrooms, or chicken, and store in an airtight container. This makes a bulk version, so tape the instructions on your container so they'll be easily accessible when the time comes.

To make the equivalent of one can of cream soup: mix ⅓ cup dry soup with 1¼ cups water. Bring to a gentle boil over medium heat and cook for 3–4 minutes or until thickened. Add celery, mushrooms, or chicken. Stir constantly so that soup will not burn or stick to bottom of pan.

Quick Pancake Mix

If you have a family tradition of making pancakes every Saturday morning, or you would like to start such a family tradition, you will find this basic recipe very helpful.

16 cups	all-purpose flour (you may use half whole wheat flour)
⅔ cup	baking powder
1½ Tbsp.	cream of tartar
⅓ cup	sugar
2 Tbsp.	salt
3 cups	powdered milk
3 Tbsp.	cinnamon

Mix all together and store in an airtight container. Yields 20 cups.

When you want to make pancakes: beat 2 eggs, and add 1¼ cups milk. Stir in about 2 cups of dry mixture just until blended. Fry on hot griddle until lightly browned on each side. Makes approximately 12 pancakes per recipe. If pancakes are too thick for your liking, add additional milk in tablespoon increments until you get your desired consistency.

> **And Another Thing . . . And Another Thing . . .** For variety, add chopped apples, pecans, or blueberries to the batter. Also, if you made the recipe with half wheat flour, you will need to add an additional ½ cup of milk when you mix up your batter.

Homemade Cheese Sauce

I like to use this in place of canned cheese sauce when we are having Mexican food. In cooking, my goal is to use as little processed food as possible. This cheese sauce has been a work in progress.

1½ Tbsp.	salted butter, melted
1½ Tbsp.	flour
1½ cups	half-and-half
1½ cups	cheddar cheese, shredded
4 oz.	cream cheese, cubed
pinch	salt
	cayenne pepper (optional)

In a heavy saucepan over medium heat, melt butter and stir in flour. Cook for 1 minute, stirring constantly. Gradually whisk in half-and-half. Simmer on low until sauce is thickened, about 5 minutes. Do not allow to boil. Remove from heat and whisk in cheddar cheese and cream cheese; stir until melted and smooth. Season with salt and cayenne pepper, if desired. Serve immediately. Yields 2 cups.

> **And Another Thing . . . And Another Thing . . .** I have found that the key to making this sauce is to add the cheese slowly, and also to make sure that the mixture is not too hot when you're adding the cheese. If it is really hot, let milk mixture cool a bit before adding the cheese.

If you can some of your garden goods in glass jars, be sure to save the canning lids. You can reuse them if they are not dinged up too much and the rubber seal looks good. However, please note that reusing canning lids is not recommended by the USDA. Following health and safety guidelines when canning helps ensure a quality, safe product.

That said, this past summer was the first time I ever reused my lids—and every single item I canned with reused lids successfully SEALED. I did my happy dance, because I was a skeptic. This makes my canning excursions even less expensive, and is another way to compensate for all the time I put into it.

Homemade Chocolate Syrup

I wanted to remove all foods with high fructose corn syrup from our house, but I could not imagine life without chocolate milk. Here is a great substitution. While it has sugar in it, children's little bodies can digest that easier than high fructose corn syrup.

1 cup	cocoa powder
3 cups	raw or white sugar
2 cups	hot water
½ tsp.	salt
1 Tbsp.	vanilla extract

Place cocoa powder, sugar, and water in a medium saucepan. Mix together until smooth and then heat over medium heat until boiling. Reduce heat immediately because this mixture can boil over. Boil for 5 minutes, stirring frequently. Remove from heat. Add salt and vanilla. Once cool, pour into a container that has a spout so you can easily pour it into your milk. To serve, mix about 1 tablespoon (more or less to your liking) to 1 cup cold milk. Stores in refrigerator for 4–6 months. Yields 1 quart syrup.

Easy Fruit and Vegetable Rinse

Children really do learn by observing the things that go on around them. I am seeing this as I watch my three-year-old. He recently has started asking me if the fruit he is about to eat has been washed before he takes a bite. I guess I have drilled into him that there are a lot of "yuckies" on fruit before it's washed. We wash raspberries, strawberries, apples, cabbage . . . everything with this simple, inexpensive solution. This helps to wash away some of the pesticides/herbicides used on produce in addition to all the dirt from hands that may have touched the produce during transportation.

32 oz.	hydrogen peroxide (3 percent solution)
	spray bottle

Pour peroxide into spray bottle. Solution is ready to use immediately.

Cooked Vanilla Pudding Mix

This is a very simple recipe to make without all the added sugar and preservatives that come in boxes of vanilla pudding mix. I purchase my vanilla beans from www.topvanilla.com.

2 whole	vanilla beans
¾ cup	nonfat powdered milk
¾ cup	cornstarch
1 cup	raw or white sugar
2 tsp.	salt

With a knife, slice down the center of each vanilla bean lengthwise and scrape out the seeds. A teaspoon works great to help pull the seeds out of the pod. Be sure to break up the little clumps of seeds that form. If the seeds appear moist or damp, allow to dry for several hours on your countertop. In a large mixing bowl combine vanilla bean seeds, powdered milk, cornstarch, sugar, and salt. Place in a glass quart jar and store in a cool, dry place.

To make pudding, combine ½ cup vanilla mixture with 2 cups cold milk in a saucepan. Whisk over medium-high heat, stirring constantly. Bring to a boil, reduce heat, and cook for 3 more minutes, stirring constantly so that the pudding won't scorch. Pour into little glass bowls. Serve warm or cold. If you chill the pudding before serving, put plastic wrap on top of the warm pudding so that a film doesn't form over the pudding.

Dishwasher Rinse Agent

1 Tbsp.	vinegar

Place the vinegar in the reservoir in your dishwasher where you would normally place the rinse agent.

Laundry Soap

Don't despair if you look in the laundry soap aisle of your grocery store and don't find all of these ingredients. Not every grocery store carries these items, so you may have to look at another local grocery or department store.

1 (5½ oz.)	Fels-Naptha laundry bar
2 cups	water
1 cup	Borax
1 cup	Arm & Hammer super washing soda
4 gallon	bucket with a lid
several drops	lavender essential oil (optional)

Grate Fels-Naptha into a cooking kettle. Add water and heat until soap is dissolved. Remove from heat and pour into bucket. Add Borax and super washing soda and stir until dissolved. Add enough water to fill the bucket completely. Stir thoroughly. Add essential oil, if using. Let set until cool. Once cool, the soap will gel up a bit. Either use your hand or take a spoon and stir to break up gel. Place lid on bucket and store. Add ⅓ cup to each load of laundry. I estimate it costs me $2.45 plus a little bit of time to make a 4-gallon bucket of laundry soap that will clean my family's clothes for 6–8 weeks.

Window Cleaner

6 Tbsp.	vinegar
3 cups	water
1	spray bottle

Mix together vinegar and water. Pour into spray bottle and use as you would use any glass cleaner. It costs pennies to make this.

> And Another Thing . . . And Another Thing . . . Instead of using paper towels to wash your windows, use newspaper. I know it seems odd but it is a great way to recycle some of those old newspapers, and they clean windows better than paper towels, with fewer streaks.

Author's Note

I am not a purist in the truest form when it comes to clearing my pantry of convenience foods. However, I do attempt to use as many basic, natural, organic, and wholesome products as I can, ones that don't have additives, food dyes, or preservatives in them. In this book, you will find that I do call on convenience foods at times. Sometimes we need something to make our jobs a bit easier when we are in a pinch! The basics that I never compromise on are always real butter, olive oil, white wheat flour, yogurt, aluminum-free baking powder, sea salt, good whole milk, chicken stock, and beef stock. You can create a lot of yummy food with these few ingredients!

The ingredients I choose to stay away from for the most part are high fructose corn syrup (which suppresses your appetite and is often found in highly nonnutritional foods), food dyes, hydrogenated oils (which are difficult for your body to digest), baking powder with aluminum, ultra pasteurized dairy products (ultra pasteurization kills good and bad bacteria in dairy products), MSG, and nitrates (found as a preservative in most deli meats, ham, and bacon).

I am not a nutritionist, but I learned many things while I owned The Farmer's Wife, mainly from customers with health problems who gave me my education in what had caused their illnesses. I am so grateful for what I have learned from those interactions.

Recipe Index

Recipe Index

Dawn Stoltzfus compiled her collection of recipes while living at home as a dairy farmer's daughter, when traveling domestically and internationally, and while operating her own business. She grew up in a real farmhouse kitchen where she had the opportunity to create recipes for her family of six at a young age, when her mother gave her the responsibility of cooking dinner one night a week. Her love for cooking was developed through their busy lives of running a farm. At the end of the day they were all hungry and ready to eat good, wholesome food! Her family raised its own beef, had fresh milk, and had a brood of chickens her mother named and gathered eggs from.

Dawn opened and managed The Farmer's Wife, a small bakery, deli, and bulk food store, until her two boys came along. Currently, she lives in Catlett, Virginia, a tiny, western suburb of Washington, DC. She is married to Merv, who is not a farmer but has milked cows in his lifetime. He enjoys the country-fresh air with her. She has two sweet, rambunctious little boys and a precious baby girl she loves to spend her days with.

Read her blog at www.dawnstoltzfus.com